CONTENTS

CRIME AND ECONOMY

11th Criminological
Colloquium
(1994)

OPENING ADDRESS

by
Mr M. JOUTSEN
General Rapporteur,
European Institute
for Crime Prevention and Control,
affiliated with the United Nations (HEUNI)
(Finland)

1.   Introduction

1.1.   The topic of the Eleventh Criminological Colloquium, «Crime and Economy», is concerned with the links between structural economic changes and business cycles, and crime. This provides scope for a discussion on a wide range of problems, ranging from the possible relationships between poverty and crime, and the impact of economic recession on ethnic violence, to the criminogenic effects of a transition from a planned economy to a free market economy. Such a topic is highly timely for the member states of the Council of Europe.

1.2.   Western Europe is slowly beginning to recover from a long recession. In most Western European countries, the annual economic growth rate currently ranges from one to three percent, and inflation is around five percent. Most national unemployment figures range between five and ten percent, although in some countries (Spain and Ireland) unemployment has soared to almost twenty percent. The unemployment figures for certain demographic groups (such as for young males in urban areas, a group that is a central concern in criminal policy) can be much higher.

The twelve member states of the European Union — perhaps to be joined by four more at the beginning of 1995 — have agreed to remove international barriers to the free movement of persons, goods, services and capital. This will create a new basis for economic development, and will require considerable regional restructuring of economic activity. People will seek better economic opportunities not only in other parts of their own country, but in other member states of the European Union. They are being joined by an increasing stream of economic refugees and migrants from Eastern Europe, North Africa and other regions.

1.3.   The «countries in transition» in Central and Eastern Europe are shifting from a centrally planned economy to a free market economy. Almost throughout this region, the indicators during the early 1990s have shown that the (official) economy not only has not grown, it has in fact shrunk. Earlier, prices had been kept artificially low through a combination of central planning and enormous subsidies. Poorly managed industries could survive because of the absence of competition. When free enterprise was allowed, such industries were no longer viable because of the increase in the price of raw materials, the demand for increased wages, and the sudden appearance of both domestic and foreign competition.

This sudden transformation of the economy has led, for the first time in memory, to wide-spread unemployment and (officially recognised) rapid inflation. For example in Poland, the number of unemployed persons jumped from 56,000 in January 1990 to 1,300,000 in March 1991 (Moskalewicz and Swiatkiewicz, p. 97). In Romania, the number of unemployed persons increased from some 20,000 in 1991 to 500,000 in mid-1992, with a predicted increase to 1,000,000 at the end of 1992, out of a total population of 24,000,000 (Romanian Embassy in Helsinki; verbal communication 7 September 1992). The annual rate of inflation in some countries can exceed 100 %; in 1991, the estimated annual rate for Lithuania was 200 % and for Bulgaria 420 %.

7

The economic transformation in the Central and Eastern European has required the drafting of new legislation and the development of new supervisory mechanisms. This new legislation must cover such matters as product safety; the licensing of enterprises engaged in certain sectors of the economy (such as financial institutions); monopolies and state control of enterprises producing certain services or products (such as alcohol); regulation of marketing practices in order to safeguard fair competition and protect employees and consumers; and state subsidies to stabilise or promote structural change. Where supervision of this new legislation has remained ineffective, unrestricted market forces may be leading not to a free market, but to what has more aptly been called a wild market, and to the growth of economic and organised crime.

The smoothness of the economic transition has varied considerably from one Central and Eastern European country to the next. Countries such as Hungary and Slovenia, which have had a longer period of adjustment, have had less severe disruptions than, for example, Bulgaria, the Czech Republic or Romania. There are also considerable differences in the strength of the underground economy and in the overall approach to economic transition, for example in respect to openness to foreign ownership of industries and to the speed and scope of privatisation. For this reason, the countries of Central and Eastern Europe should not be regarded as a homogenous group from the point of view of the topic.

2.   Theories regarding the links between crime and the economy

2.1.   Since the economy is a major determinant of social structures and social relationships, the economic development and integration in Western Europe and the transition to a free market economy in Central and Eastern Europe presumably has affected and will continue to affect the structure and amount of crime. The reports to the Eleventh Criminological Colloquium have been designed to stimulate a discussion on what these effects may be, and if possible on how the negative consequences can be avoided or minimised. The framework for the discussion will deal with the long-term structural economic changes, business cycles, opportunity theory, and the impact of economic change on the structure and operation of the criminal justice system itself.

The long-term economic development (during the 1800s and the 1900s) has led to urbanisation, the expansion of state authority, more pervasive social relations, a need for greater self-control and discipline, and changes in values. Economic and social changes after World War II have led not only to a higher general standard of living, but also to the emergence of new urban underclasses, immigration, poverty and social deprivation.

Long-term structural economic changes set the stage; in the shorter term, business cycles set the mood. During the present century, much of Europe has undergone clear business cycles of growth and decay, boom and bust. Growth brings with it higher employment, a higher standard of living and a general mood of optimism; recession brings lost jobs, a lower standard of living and frustrated hopes. The recession that hit Europe at the end of the 1980s came after a lengthy period of growth, when the new generations had learned to take high employment and a higher standard of living almost for granted. The recession has brought both the individual and the welfare state face-to-face with economic reality.

2.2.   Perhaps the most familiar hypothesis linking crime and the economy is that unemployment and economic inequality increase the amount of crime. The common-sense reasoning is that persons (often young males) who are out of work and thus not earning a living have the time and motive to commit both planned crime (for financial gain) and impulse crime (such as crimes of violence after bouts of drinking). Economic inequality, in turn, creates feelings of relative deprivation, which can increase the motivation to commit offences.

A more refined version of this hypothesis was first presented by Becker (1968; see also Ehrlich 1973), who hypothesised that if the certainty and severity of punishment are held constant, an increase in the potential rewards from crime and a decrease in the costs of participation in crime (such as time lost from work) will increase the amount of crime. Unemployment lowers the costs of participation in crime, and income inequality increases the perceived potential rewards (Stack 1984).

2.3.   A related line of thinking is the «opportunity theory». An expanded economy generates more wealth and different time use patterns, and thus increases the opportunity for crime. For example, a higher standard of living brings with it more consumer goods, and people may go out more during their leisure time. An expanding economy also brings more women into the labour force, and residential areas are left unsupervised (Cohen 1981, Mukherjee 1986). In times of recession, in turn, persons who become unemployed will tend to spend more time at home, increasing guardianship of their property and decreasing the opportunity for crime (Cohen, Felson and Land 1980; but see Cook and Zarkin 1985).

2.4.   Economic development and underdevelopment are linked not only to the amount of crime, but also to the *structure* of crime. An increasingly complex economy creates new types of crime, such as those identified in Recommendation No. R (81) 12 of the Committee of Ministers to member states on economic crime. An underdeveloped economy that fails to meet consumer demand may be challenged by an alternative (underground) economy, which in itself increases crime. State intervention in the economy, in turn, may be criminogenic, for example by creating the opportunity for subsidy fraud, tax fraud, smuggling in order to avoid tariffs, and currency speculation.

The organisers of the Eleventh Criminological Colloquium wish the focus of the discussions to be on the links between the economy and crime, and not on economic crime per se, a subject that has already received separate consideration (Economic Crime 1981). It is understood that no fine distinction can be made between these two closely intertwined topics. It has been pointed out, for example, that during a recession, businesses may try to stay solvent by engaging in such economic crime as fraudulent bankruptcies and credit fraud. During times of rapid economic growth, bogus firms may be established to attract speculators. Nonetheless, the participants are requested to bear in mind that economic crime is only one narrow aspect of the topic under discussion.

3. Theories regarding the links between crime control and the economy

A separate line of inquiry, which enlarges the topic of the Eleventh Criminological Colloquium, moves from «crime and economy» to «crime control and economy». The state of the economy may affect both the operation and the severity of the criminal justice system.

On the individual level, first of all, the economy may affect the perception that criminal justice authorities have regarding the dangerousness of offenders. In particular, if a sentencing judge normally regards an unemployed offender as more dangerous than an employed offender, he or she may change this perception during times of mass unemployment.

On a more general level, it may be hypothesised that the criminal justice system may attempt to react to the social unrest caused by a recession (or provide the unrest with a legitimate channel of expression) by increasing the severity of punishment in order to hold in check the «army of the unemployed». This social unrest may well be manifested as ethnic violence; «outsiders» are commonly blamed for taking jobs away from the local population.

The economy may also affect the unit of punishment or the assessment of the seriousness of different offences. For example, a higher standard of living and a greater value on time increases the relative punitiveness of a sentence of imprisonment, just as it increases the practicability of a fine as punishment. A higher standard of living, in turn, may change public perceptions regarding the relative seriousness of personal and property crime. These changed perceptions will affect, for example, reporting to the police, and the demand for punishment.

Finally, the criminal justice system itself is subject to economic laws. During recessions, when tax revenues fall off, the criminal justice system, from the police through to corrections, is under pressure to do more with less; it must improve its own working and management methods in order to be able to deal with increasing caseloads. Police patrolling may be curtailed and police stations may be closed, criminal proceedings may be simplified so that prosecutors and judges can deal with more cases, and rehabilitation programmes may be discontinued. Crime prevention schemes, which do not ordinarily produce results that would satisfy efficiency experts, may well remain unfunded.

Despite the economic crunch throughout Europe, however, the criminal justice system may prove much more resilient than for example private enterprise. Some have claimed that criminal justice constitutes a self-perpetuating system. For example Nils Christie (1993) has pointed out the economic (industrial) interest in the expansion of the criminal justice system. The criminal justice system itself creates a large number of jobs, it has a strong political backing, it requires large investments and it fulfills basic social functions. The fear of crime can be and is readily used to argue for expanded criminal justice, and for a more punitive approach to crime. The economy, crime and crime control are inextricably intermeshed.

BIBLIOGRAPHY

Becker, G.S. (1968), Crime and punishment: An economic approach, in Journal of Political Economy, vol. 78, pp. 526-536

Cohen, L.E. (1981), Modeling Crime Trends: A Criminal Opportunity Perspective, Journal of Research in Crime and Delinquency, vol. 18, pp. 138-164

Cohen, L.F., M. Felson and K.C. Land (1980), Property Crime Rates in the United States: A Macrodynamic Analysis, 1947-1977; with Ex-Ante Forecast for the Mid-1980s, American Journal of Sociology, vol. 86, pp. 90-118

Christie, Nils (1993), Crime Control as Industry, Routledge, London and New York

Cook, P.J. and G.A. Zarkin (1985), Crime and the Business Cycle, Journal of Legal Studies, vol. 14, pp. 115-128

Economic Crime (1981), European Committee on Crime Problems, Strasbourg

Ehrlich, I. (1973), Participation in illegitimate activities: A theoretical and empirical investigation, in Journal of Political Economy, vol. 81, pp. 521-565

Moskalewicz, Jacek and Grazyna Swiatkiewicz, Social problems in the Polish political debate, in Jussi Simpura and Christoffer Tigerstedt, Social Problems Around the Baltic Sea, Nordic Council for Alcohol and Drug Research publication no. 21, Helsinki 1992, pp. 85-108

Mukherjee, S.K. (1986), Economic Development and Crime: A Case of Burglary, International Annals of Criminology, vol. 24, pp. 237-253

Stack, S. (1984) Income Inequality and Property Crime: A Cross-National Analysis of Relative Deprivation Theory, Criminology, vol. 22, pp. 229-237

CRIME AND ECONOMY

11th Criminological
Colloquium
(1994)

THE EFFECTS
OF ECONOMIC STRUCTURES
AND PHASES OF DEVELOPMENT ON CRIME

by
Mr M. EISNER
Chair of Sociology,
Swiss Federal Institute of Technology,
Zurich
(Switzerland)

CONTENTS

1.   Introduction

There is an abundance of ways in which socio-economic structures may be thought to be related to crime and its different manifestations. This paper is restricted to one perspective. It discusses the question of how long-term changes in the socio-economic structure of modern societies have – or have not – influenced trends in crime rates as measured by available indicators.

In the first part of this paper (section 2) I discuss three criminological theories that make different assumptions about the effects of long-term socio-economic change on trends in crime rates. Criminological *modernisation theory, opportunity theory* and the *theory of the civilizing process* will be treated as theories based on the assumption that crime rates should either increase or decrease as the level of economic production rises.

In the second part of the paper I present empirical evidence regarding homicide rates and overall crime rates in a number of European countries which confirm the U-shaped pattern expected by Gurr (1981) for Western societies. Based on this evidence I argued that neither of the theoretical models discussed yield a satisfactory explanation of observable empirical trends.

In the third part of the paper I develop a tentative model that might reconciliate empirical patterns with theoretical arguments.

In the final section I discuss the question of what type of socio-economic structure is likely to emerge in the Eastern European countries and what effects this might have on the evolution of their crime rates.

2.   Long-term socio-economic trends and their effects on crime

Over the past 200 years all Western societies have experienced dramatic transformations of their economic, social and political structures which have had effects on almost every aspect of everyday life. There have been many efforts to conceptually organise the evidence of these changes and to develop theories that can explain what has changed. While some approaches, e.g., *modernisation theory*, the theory of the civilizing process, have given greater weight to evolutionary trends others, e.g., World-system theory, long-wave theory, have rather emphasised discontinuities and cyclical aspects of social change. Within this paper I restrict myself to trend models of long-term socio-economic change.

One of the most influential approaches to theoretically understanding long-term trends of social change over the last 200 years is modernisation theory (Aron, 1962; Lerner, 1964; Lipset, 1963; So, 1990). Following general classical theories of, e.g., Ferdinand Tönnies, Emile Durkheim, Talcott Parsons, modernisation theory is based on the assumption that the experiences of Western societies since the onset of the Industrial Revolution can be understood as a universal transition from *tradition* to *modernity* accompanied by law-like patterns of socio-economic, cultural and political change.

Although more recent research has shown that modernisation theory has overstressed the universalities of the modernisation process there is no doubt that Western European countries have shared some very fundamental processes of long-term social change during the past 200 years.

Probably the most fundamental economic characteristic is the transition to *sustained economic growth* after the Industrial Revolutions that took place between the late 18th and the mid 19th centuries in most European countries (Rostow, 1960). The notion of sustained economic growth implies that despite oscillations economic productivity largely follows a secular growth path. For illustrative purposes figure 1 shows the development of the real gross national product in Britain between 1830 and 1990.

Figure 1   *Real Gross National Product in Britain, 1830–1990*

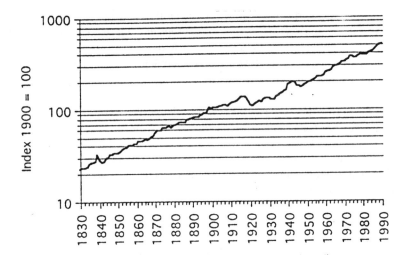

Sources: Rescaled data on the basis of Mitchell (1980) for the period 1830–1975 and OECD (1992:48) for the period 1976–1990.

This process of economic growth was accompanied by *shifts in the sectoral distribution of labour*. While economies were almost exclusively based in the agricultural sector at the beginning of the industrial take-off they transformed themselves into – first – industrial and later postindustrial economies with an expanding service sector.

Urbanisation too has been a universal co-variate of socio-economic modernisation with all European countries becoming transformed from predominantly rural to predominantly urban societies. Also, driven by the stepwise introduction of new transport technologies, levels of *spatial mobility* have increased exponentially over the last 200 years.

A variety of political, social and cultural changes have been found to co-vary with economic modernisation. To name only a few I mention the *expansion of state activities*, the *demographic revolution* including rising expectations of life, the *growth of general educational levels* and increasing *individualisation* and *secularisation* (see, e.g., Flora et al., 1983; Meyer, 1980).

It is a highly plausible assumption that these profound transformations of European socio-economic structures during the past 200 years have had some influence on crime. The question difficult to answer is: *what* influence? Two radically diverging hypotheses have been discussed in the literature. The criminological variant of modernisation theory as well as criminological opportunity theory assume that socio-economic modernisation causes *increasing* crime, but the explanations offered for this hypothesis differ. In contrast, the criminological variant of the theory of the civilising process assumes that socio-economic modernisation causes *decreasing* crime, especially decreasing violent crime.

2.1 The disintegrating effects of economic growth and modernisation

Criminological modernisation theory is among the most widely used theoretical approaches to interpret the effects of socio-economic change on crime. Some of its prominent proponents are Marshall B. Clinard (1964; Clinard und Abbott, 1973), Howard Zehr (1976) and Louise I. Shelley (1981; 1986). In Europe criminological modernisation theory has been applied to patterns of crime development in, e.g., France and Germany (Zehr, 1976), Yugoslavia (Zvekic, 1994), Sweden (Wikström, 1991). Switzerland (Clinard, 1978) has been discussed as an exception to the general rule that affluence, industrialisation, and urbanisation are accompanied by increasing crime rates.

Following Durkheim (1983; 1988; 1991) the "modernisation and crime" model suggests that industrialisation and urbanisation generate increasing crime because of higher levels of anomie, a breakdown of social bonds, greater impersonality, a reduction of social integration and individual disorientation (Shelley, 1981: 22ff). The most fundamental tenet of criminological modernisation theory consists of four interrelated propositions regarding the effects of economic and social modernisation on the level and structure of crime (Thome, 1992) .

(1)   At the initial phases of modernisation both property and violent crime are expected to increase fast mainly because mass migration into the growing cities causes the breakdown of more traditional structures of social integration and control.

(2)   In later stages of the process of socio-economic modernisation violent crimes are expected to decline while property crimes should continue to increase. It is argued that violent crimes are primarily associated with the conditions of rural life, whereas property crimes are expected to become the dominant form of criminality in all modernising societies because tangible goods become more highly valued and more widely visible and accessible (Shelley, 1981: 139) .

(3)   Modernisation is assumed to generate rising overall crime rates, crime being an inevitable cost of socio-economic modernisation (see, e.g., Clinard and Abbott, 1973; Shelley, 1981: 137) .

(4)   The structure and rate of crime is expected to converge over time as nations converge in their economic and social structure.

As regards overall crime rates this theoretical model amounts to the hypothesis that there is a positive linear relationship between the process of modernisation and crime levels. Urbanisation and its assumed side-effects – social isolation, social disorganisation, lack of social control, anomie – are considered as the main *intervening* variables linking economic growth and increasing crime.

2.2   The growth of delinquent opportunities in expanding economies

Changing opportunity structures had already been taken into account in early formulations of criminological modernisation theory. Only since the late 1970s, however, approaches focusing on the situational dimension of crime came to be regarded as a distinct theory. The basic assumption of theoretical approaches such as the "life style model" (Hindelang, et al., 1978) and the "routine activity approach" (Cohen, 1981; Cohen und Felson, 1979; Felson, 1987; Felson and Cohen, 1980; Wikström, 1990) holds, that crimes occur when motivated offenders converge in time and space with suitable targets in the absence of capable guardians (see also van Dijk, 1994a). Furthermore, Cohen and Felson (1979) assume that the existence of motivated offenders can be regarded as constant and irrelevant for changes in crime rates. The main variables influencing differences and changes in crime rates are the availability of suitable targets and the absence of capable guardians. Crime levels are expected to be positively related to economic prosperity (van Dijk, 1990). Two arguments are offered to explain this hypothesis. First, economic growth results in an increasing abundance of durable consumer goods like, e.g. electronic equipment, cars, motorcycles which is equivalent to a higher availability of targets. Second, patterns of everyday life, e.g. more leisure time activities, less time spent at home, change as a result of socio-economic growth and thereby produce less informal control and more opportunities for delinquent acts.

As far as *property crimes* are concerned, the implications of the routine activity approach regarding the effects of long-term economic expansion are quite straight-forward. The increasing availability of consumer goods and the decline of informal social control should lead to increasing property crime (van Dijk, 1994b). The implications of the *routine activity* approach for violent crime are less clear-cut. On the one hand, increasing leisure time could contribute to more potentially violent encounters between strangers. Growing economic wealth, however, also is a resource that produces distances between individuals thereby lowering the likelihood of violent conflict between family members (see, e.g. Wikström, 1992; 1985).

Although theoretical approaches focusing on opportunity structures are mostly used in cross-sectional research, the routine activity approach has also been used to explain the trends of crime rates in, e.g., the US (Cohen und Felson, 1979), Sweden (Stack, 1982) and Britain (Field, 1990) as well as in internationally comparative studies (Bennett, 1991; LaFree and Kick, 1983; 1986; van Dijk, 1992; 1994b).

2.3 Increasing external and internal controls as a result of the expansion of capitalism

A third theoretical model to be considered here suggests that crime and especially violent crime should decrease along with the formation of modern states and the expansion of modern capitalist economies. This model is mainly based on the work of Norbert Elias (1976) and his theory of the civilizing process. It has received increasing attention since empirical work on historical crime patterns in pre-modern Europe showed extraordinarily high levels of everyday violence in Medieval societies with evidence suggesting a gradual decrease of the frequency of homicides over the following centuries (Beattie, 1974; Becker, 1976; Berents, 1985; Hammer, 1978; Hanawalt, 1976; Henry, 1984; Lagrange, 1993; Österberg und Lindström, 1988; Stone, 1983; see Gurr, 1981 for a review of the evidence).

Most criminological theories relying on Elias and his theory of the civilizing process have emphasised the interplay between (1) growing external formal control related to the formation of the state monopoly of power; (2) increasing self-control initially restricted to the social and cultural elite; (3) the gradual diffusion of both external control and self-control from the social center to the periphery (Gurr, 1981: 341).

It is important to note, however, that the *expansion of capitalism* plays an important role in the theoretical argument developed by Elias. He argues that the expansion of capitalist modes of production and exchange produced an unprecedented degree of functional differentiation in modernising societies. Its consequence is an increasing level of mutual interdependency which has to function in the absence of intensive personal knowledge. *Intensified self-control* therefore becomes a crucial social and cultural resource necessary for successful participation in a modernising society (Elias, 1976: Bd. 2, 337, 387). He argues that capitalism has contributed to the decline of interpersonal violence because – first – interpersonal violence is highly dysfunctional for the operation of markets based on mutual trust and – second – a higher degree of self-control and rationality is an important cultural resource for successful participation in capitalist markets and modern urban societies. This type of argument has been elaborated even earlier by Max Weber, who argued that the expansion of capitalism is partly to be understood as a consequence of a cultural model based on higher levels of rationalised self-control (Weber, 1920).

The theoretical argument developed by Elias has mainly been used to explain trends in violent crimes both in pre-modern and modern times (Chesnais, 1981; 1992; Franke, 1994; Gurr, 1981; Lagrange, 1993; Rousseaux, 1993). Rather little research has been done to test its applicability to trends in property crimes (but see Gurr, 1976; Gurr, et al., 1977) although the concept of self-control (see, e.g., Gottfredson und Hirschi, 1990) is now increasingly being regarded as a possible basis for a general theory of crime.

3. Long-term trends of crime in Western Europe

The discussion of theoretical models aimed at linking long-term socio-economic development and crime shows wide divergences as concerns the expected patterns of crime rates over longer historical periods. The empirical question is: what can be said about trends in European crime rates over the last 150 years and how do they relate to patterns of long-term socio-economic change. In the following section I will present an overview of some empirical data concerning trends in crime rates. I will start with presenting data on *homicide rates* in seven European countries. In a second part I will discuss empirical evidences of *total crime rates* since the first half of the 19th century. In order to give a more detailed view on more recent trends, data on police recorded crimes between 1950 and 1992, will be presented for six European countries.

3.1 Empirical trends in European homicide rates, 1800–1992

I start with a discussion of trends in homicide rates. Homicide data are generally assumed to be less vulnerable to changes in data gathering procedures than other crime indicators (see, e.g. Gartner, 1990). In historical comparisons, however, one has to bear in mind that rather little is known about the effects of, e.g., changes in classification techniques, recording practices, improved medical facilities (see, e.g., Franke, 1994; Sessar, 1981) or the statistical distortions caused by secular changes of the age-structure in modernising societies[1]. Figures 2a through 2e present data on long-term developments of homicide rates in seven European countries.

The data for *England and Wales* are conviction rates from 1832 to 1856 presented by Gatrell (1980) and homicides registered by the police from then onwards. The data for *Sweden* are five year averages of homicide rates recorded in the vital statistics and presented in von Hofer (1985). World Health Organisation data have been added from 1984 onwards. Data for *France* are based on the number of persons charged for murder and manslaughter compiled by Chesnais (1981: 53). Data for *Belgium* are victims of homicide tabulated in the "Annuaire Statistique du Belgique". For *The Netherlands*, Franke (1994) has compiled data on convictions for murder and manslaughter from 1850 to 1989 as well as data on victims of homicide from 1911 to 1989. While the data are almost identical between 1911 and 1970, there is some divergence afterwards. I used conviction data until 1970 and victim data afterwards[2]. The data for *Italy* are based on the number of crimes, for which the judicial authorities have initiated legal action. These data show considerable differences in level from those of the Italian vital statistics as shown in the WHO-yearbook between 1945 and 1990. Throughout the post World War 2 period the data presented in the police statistics are 2.3 times higher than those presented in the death statistics. This is due to the fact that police data also include attempted homicides[3]. In order to gain as much comparability as possible with the other series, original data have been rescaled by division through 2.3. Swiss data are based on unpublished tables of the national vital statistics (see Eisner, 1994; Killias, 1991; Storz, 1991) .

22

Figures 2a to 2g   Homicide rates in six European countries

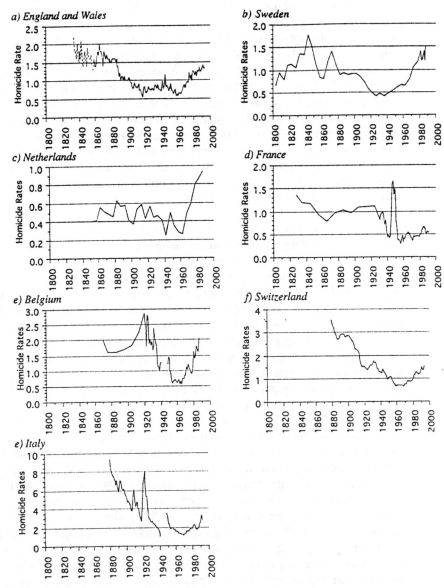

Sources and Notes:

England and Wales	1834–1856	Offences tried, see Gatrell (1980), Appendix A.
	1857–1992	Offences known to the police, Home Office
Sweden	1800–1987	Victims of Homicide, 5-years averages, see von Hofer (1985).
France	1825–1952	Persons accused of murder or manslaughter, 10-years averages, see Chesnais (1981).
	1953–1975	Persons convicted of murder or manslaughter, see Chesnais (1981).
Belgium	1860–1987	Victims of homicide, 1860–1920 10-years averages, 1970, annual data. Annuaire statistique de la Belgique, several years.
Italy	1881–1992	Homicides reported to the police, ISTAT.
Switzerland	1876–1991	Victims of homicide, Todesursachenstatistik, unpublished tables.

23

Data on *England and Wales* show a stable level of homicides between the 1830s and the 1860s. From then onwards a declining trend prevails until c.1920. From the 1920s to the 1960s homicide rates remain stable and from the mid 1960s an increasing trend can be observed. The U-shaped pattern can also be observed for police recorded assaults confirming its validity as an indicator of secular trends in violent crime (Gatrell, 1980). Sweden is the only country on which data stretch back until 1750. The data presented here show that there has been an increase of homicide rates until the 1840s which started c.1800 (von Hofer, 1991). From then until the 1920s homicide rates declined by a factor of 3. After World War 2 homicide rates start to increase. The level observed in the 1980s is quite similar to the one observed 150 years earlier. *French* data suggest a slowly declining trend from the 1820s until the late 1950s interrupted by a short increase shortly after WW2. A secular trough in the late 1950s is followed be a gradual increase in the following period.

Contrary to the declining trend prevailing in most other series considered here, homicide rates in *Belgium* have increased until approx. 1910. It is interesting to note, however, that neighbouring Germany also has experienced an increase of homicide rates between c.1880 to 1914 followed by a gradual decline until the mid 1950s (Chesnais, 1981). From c.1920 until the mid 1960s a steep decrease can be observed followed by a symmetrical increase until the late 1980s. Levels of homicide rates were already very low in *the Netherlands* around the 1850s but decreased somewhat until the 1960s. From then onwards a considerable increase has occurred. Both *Italy* and *Switzerland* have very similar long-term trends in homicide rates although levels are higher in Italy than in Switzerland. In both countries homicide rates have declined by a factor of approximately five between the 1880 and the 1960s. From the mid 1960s onwards both countries have experienced a considerable increase in homicide rates.

Data available for some countries suggest that the decreases of total homicide-rates were mainly due to – first – the decline of the number of *male victims* with the sex-ratio of victims falling from approx. 5:1 in the 1870s to 1:1 in the 1950s in Belgium, Sweden and Switzerland (see Killias, 1991: 124; von Hofer, 1991: 31) and – second – the reduction of *infanticides* which have continuously decreased for both sexes until the present time (see, e.g., Gartner, 1990: 99; Killias, 1991: 123). The decline of infanticides is especially noteworthy from a perspective that combines rational-choice arguments (see, e.g., Niggli, 1994) with long-term socio-economic developments. Thus one may argue that the change of family structures associated with socio-economic modernisation has contributed to a greater emotional valuation of children while increasing incomes and the spread of welfare institutions have reduced the pressure to kill unwanted children[4]. The theory of the civilizing process, however, offers no explanations for the observation that the rate of *adult female* victims of homicide has not followed the overall declining trend.

As the countries for which homicide data were available represent a considerable fraction of Western Europe I considered it worthwhile to compute estimates of overall trends. The basis were average homicide rates at five year intervals for all countries excluding periods of war[5]. For the period from 1830/34 to 1985/89 a series was computed based on the unweighed averages for England and Wales, France and Sweden. For the period from 1880/84 to 1985/89 a second series based on data for all seven countries was also computed. As this second series includes countries with rather high homicide rates, e.g., Switzerland and Italy, two different scales are used to present the data in figure 3.

Figure 3   *Overall trend of homicide rates in Europe, 5-year intervals, periods of war (1914-1919 and 1939-1949) excluded*

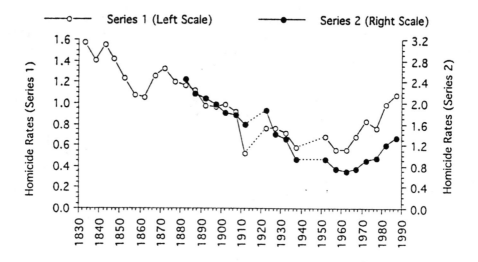

Note:
Series 1 is based on the (unweighed) averages of England and Wales, France and Sweden.
Series 2 is based on the (unweighed) averages of Belgium, England and Wales, France, Italy, the Netherlands, Sweden and Switzerland.
For sources see above, figures 2a to 2e.

These data show that the overall trend of European homicide rates follows a strikingly clear pattern. Although national data show considerable discrepancies in local trends during some sub-periods of the 19th century the trend predominating in Europe is a continuous decrease that has probably started in the 1840s and come to an end in the early 1960s. From the 1960s onwards European homicide rates have been increasing with national differences being restricted to the relative extent of the increase.

3.2   Total crime trends between 1830 and 1990

Assessing long-term trends is an even more tedious task for overall crime than for homicides which are very rare events but not all too open to variations in definition and the chance to become identified as such. The only data bases that are quite frequently available over longer periods of time concern the *number of persons convicted for criminal offences*. Difficulties for interpreting these data are abundant as there are variations in the content of criminal law, variations in the chance that crimes become known, that known crimes be cleared and that known offenders become convicted. It has been questioned whether these data can at all be interpreted as evidence indicating changes in the frequency of crime or whether they must be rather understood as indicators of the control activity of the state (see, e.g., Melossi, 1994). Following the arguments brought forward by Gurr (1976: 59ff) on this issue I will assume here that despite distortions regarding the precise extent and the exact timing of variations the available data still yield the basis for gross estimates of long-term trends.

Some of the most comprehensive figures on long-term developments of crime in Western societies have been collected by Gurr et al. (1977: 644). They computed common trends in both property crimes and violent crimes for Stockholm, London and Sydney from 1830 to 1965. I reproduce the figures shown by Gurr at al. (1977) below.

Figure 4a   *The common trend in convictions for crimes of theft and violence in London, Stockholm and Sydney (see Gurr at al., 1977, 644).*

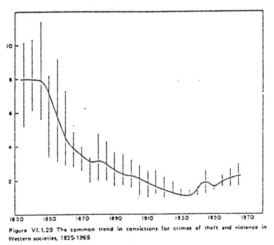

Figure VI.1.20 The common trend in convictions for crimes of theft and violence in Western societies, 1835-1965

Figure 4b   *The common trend in known crimes of theft and violence in London, Stockholm and Sydney (see Gurr at al., 1977, 644).*

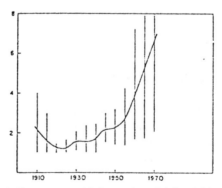

Figure VI.1.21 The common trend in known crimes of theft and violence in Western societies, 1910-1970

On conviction rates were high up to the late 1840s and declined until c.1930. From then onwards conviction rates have increased but remained well below the level observed in the early 19th century. Data on police recorded crimes suggest that the lower turning may have been around the 1920s with steep increases starting in the late 1950s. Gurr at al. (1977) conclude that the overall pattern of crime trends resembles a U-shaped pattern with the lower turing point somewhere between the 1920s and the 1950s.

The data presented by Gurr et al. (1977) include two European cities only. It is quite remarkable, however, that data on other areas in Europe tend to corroborate the secular trends found by Gurr et al. (1977).

England and Wales are probably best documented as concerns historical crime trends. Concerning the period prior to the 1850s, Emsley (1994: 151) has found sharp increases in crime from the first decade of the 19th century until about 1850. Since 1857 data on crimes recorded by the police are available. Figure 5 shows the development of crime rates on a logarithmic scale. Police recorded crime rates have declined in this country by a factor of 2:1 between 1857 and the early 1920s. From then onwards the data show an exponentially increasing trend that remains basically unbroken until the present (Maguire, 1994).

Figure 5   *Police recorded Crimes in England and Wales*

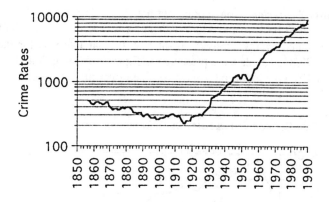

Source: Data supplied by the Home Office.

In *Italy*, data on the number of crimes for which legal action was initiated have been collected since 1880. From 1880 until the late 1930s crime rates have fluctuated with no discernible trend (see figure 6). An increasing trend can only be found after World War 2 showing an accelerated pace since c.1970. Conviction rates are available since 1890 and have decreased by about 2:1 until the 1950s when the lower turning point is reached.

Figure 6   *Crimes for which legal action was initiated in Italy*

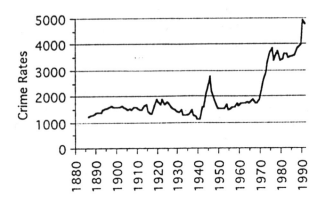

Source: Istat, Statistiche giudiziarie, several years.

Swedish rates of convictions for theft decreased considerably between the 1840s and the 1880s and remained stable up to the mid 1920s (von Hofer und Tham, 1989). From then onwards the data show a very sharp increase which has slowed down somewhat in the 1980s.

As regards *Switzerland* conviction data are available for three large cantons (Zürich, Vaud, Geneva) back to the 1830s (Eisner, 1992; Killias, 1991; Killias und Riva, 1984). I computed average conviction rates at 10-year intervals for the period from 1832/41 to 1972/81. The data are presented in figure 7. After an initial rise in the 1830s and early 1840s, conviction rates have declined over more than 120 years only to increase slightly in the 1980s.

Figure 7   *Trend of conviction rates in Switzerland, 10-year averages*

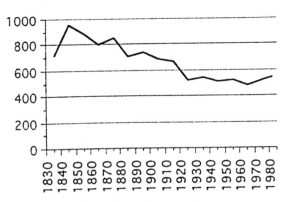

Note: Average conviction rates in the cantons of Zürich, Vaud and Geneva. Computations based on data supplied by Martin Killias for Vaud and Geneva. See Eisner (1992) for Zürich.

The Comparative Crime Data File (CCDF) compiled by Archer and Gartner (1984) contains tables on conviction rates for a number of other European countries, e.g., Ireland, Norway, Portugal Scotland over the period 1900 to 1972. Most of these series conform to the U-shaped pattern suggested by Gurr (1977, 1981) by showing the lowest rates of either violent or property crime rates between the late 1920s and the early 1950s.

It thus seems that despite the fact that conviction data are unreliable a quite universal pattern of trends may have characterised European crime rates. They indicate a decline between the 1840s and the 1920s, a trough between c.1920 and c.1950, and increases from the 1950s until the present.

3.3   Trends of police recorded crime between 1950 and 1992

Although it is commonplace by now that police data of recorded crimes have serious limitations as indicators of "real" levels of crime they are usually assumed to be superior to data on conviction rates or prison populations (Hindelang, et al., 1981; Junger-Tas, 1991). I therefore add data on police recorded crimes since 1950 to the data discussed above. However, differences in reporting levels of the population, in recording practices by local police officers, in categorisation rules and in counting practices defined by departments of statistics make comparisons of police data both over time and between countries difficult and fraught with errors (see, e.g., McClintock und Wikström, 1990; McClintock und Wikström, 1992).

All the countries reviewed here undertook revisions of their statistical data gathering techniques during the period considered here. Whereas some had the effect of lowering somewhat crime rates (e.g. exclusion of traffic-related crimes) most are usually considered to have had an increasing effect on officially published figures. Concerning violent crimes some studies have suggested that part of the general increase observed may be due to a higher tendency to report less serious crimes (e.g. Wikström, 1991) and/or a higher tendency of the police to record offences reported to them (Reiss und Roth, 1993: 413). Both effects would reduce the "real" extent of increases. However, given the general lack of victimisation surveys in Europe before the 1980s, however, data on police recorded crimes may still be regarded as a useful indicator to assess national crime trends (Junger-Tas, 1991) .

The figures presented indicate overall crime rates in those six European countries for which data were available from 1950 to 1992.

Figures 8a to 8f Total crime rates in six European countries, 1950–1992

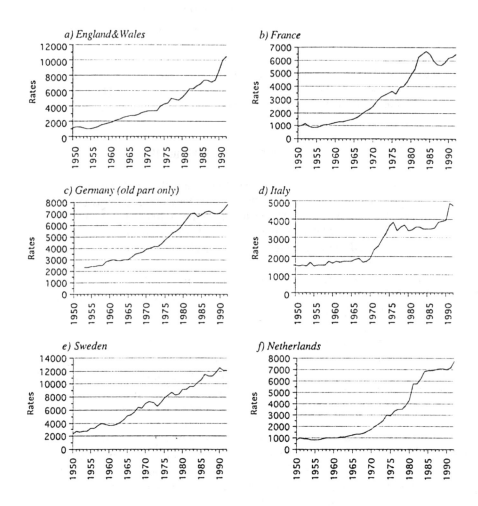

Sources:

England and Wales: Data supplied by the Home Office.
France: Adjusted series quoted in Council of Europe, Economic Crisis and
                             Crime, 1985 and Ministère de l'Intérieur, La criminalité en France.
Germany: Bundeskriminalamt (Ed.), Polizeiliche Kriminalstatistik, several
                             years.
Italy: Istat, Delitti denunciati per i quali l'Autorià giudiziaria ha inziato
                             l'azione penale.
Sweden: Statistical Yearbook of Sweden, several years.
Netherlands: Statistical Yearbook of the Netherlands, several years.

Despite some national differences, on which I will not comment here, the data show a striking degree of similarity over time. Given this similarity of the trend component I considered it worthwhile to compute (unweighed) average annual crime rates across all six countries. The data are presented in figure 9.

Figure 9   *Common Trend in police recorded crimes in six European countries*

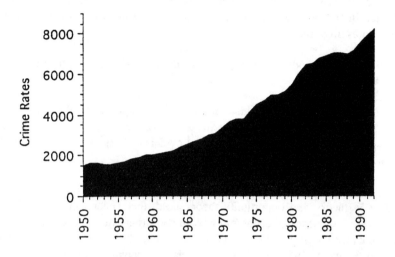

Note: Averages of the series shown in figures 8a to 8f, unweighed by population size.

The dominating feature is a strong increase from approximately 1600 crimes per 100 000 of the population in the early 50s to c. 7900 crimes in the early 90s corresponding to a fivefold rise within forty years and an average annual growth rate of approximately 4.1 percent. An analysis of mean growth rates for sub-periods shows that the increases have been somewhat lower during the 1950s and the 1980s and higher in the 1960s and 1970s.

Table 1 Growth of average crime rates in six European countries

Period	Mean annual growth rates
1951-1960	3.3 %
1961-1970	4.4 %
1971-1980	5.3 %
1981-1990	3.3 %
1951-1990	4.1 %

Note: Geometric means of annual growth rates of the series presented in figure 9.

Given that most recorded crimes are property crimes the development of overall crime rates may be assumed to be a good indicator of the development of property crimes. But, trends of violent crime rates do not seem to have differed much from the overall trend. Some quite marked differences between sub-categories may be noted. In all European countries theft of and from vehicles, robberies and criminal damages have increased at a faster pace than total crime rates. Robbery, for example, has increased at least tenfold since the early 50s in all the countries on which I was able to find data. In contrast, sexual offences, assaults and simple thefts have increased at a lower than average rate.

3.4 Theoretical models and empirical evidences on long-term trends: A critical Assessment

How do the empirical evidences concerning long-term trends in crime square with the theoretical models discussed in section 2? Without being too restrictive concerning the interpretation of the empirical evidence, I argue that neither is able to explain well the trends prevailing in Europe.

Although based on different theoretical arguments both criminological modernisation theory and opportunity theory hold, that general crime levels should increase as a consequence of economic growth and urbanisation. The few quantitative empirical data for the *first half of the 19th century* tend to confirm an increasing trend. However it is unclear whether these data reflect changes in the real frequency of criminal events or whether they are a consequence of intensified and more professionalised policing (Gatrell, 1980: 274–278). Given the scarcity and low quality of empirical data on crime trends in the first half of the 19th century, it will probably remain impossible to know whether rapid urbanisation significantly contributed to that process.

More detailed data on crime patterns in the second half of the 19th century allow for more rigorous tests of the assumed link between *urbanisation and crime*. A simple comparison of trends runs counter to the assumed relationship. While urbanisation proceeded at a fast pace during the whole of the 19th century all evidence suggest declining or at most stable crime rates until the 1920s. Rigorous empirical tests of the urbanisation-crime link on the basis of regional data have been performed by Johnson for Imperial Germany (Johnson, 1990; Johnson und McHale, 1980; McHale und Johnson, 1977) and by Lodhi and Tilly (1973) and Gillis (1989) for France in the second half of the 19th century. This empirical research has failed to show a consistent causal influence of urbanisation on crime. Neither in Imperial Germany (Johnson und McHale, 1980) nor in France (Lodhi und Tilly, 1973) or Britain (Gatrell, 1980) the process of urbanisation seems to have had an increasing impact on either property or violent crime. From the perspective of both modernisation theory and opportunity theory it might even be regarded as a paradox that the trend of rising crime rates in the 1950s started in a period when the growth of the very large cities tended to slow down and in some cases even resulted in a net loss of the population.

In support of the *routine activity approach* it is often mentioned that crime rates in most Western societies have increased largely parallel to the process of economic growth (see, e.g., van Dijk, 1994a). While this may be true for patterns prevailing since the 1950s, it does not fit the experiences before that period. There is no doubt that between the 1850s and the late 1920s economic growth resulted in gradual increases of personal incomes and some growth of the availability of consumer goods. Ordinary people in the 1920s were definitely more likely than in the 1850s to have some possessions in their homes and to have potentially attractive goods or cash with them on the streets (Emsley, 1994). Also, the widespread grievances about the anonymity of the big cities of the early 20th century (see, e.g., Simmel, 1903; Wirth, 1938) do not support the idea that informal personal control made opportunities for predatory crime very rare. Still property crimes seem either to have remained stable or even to have declined in the large cities. Summarising the empirical evidence concerning the 19th century Gatrell (1980: 238) argues, "that in many societies, historically, economic, demographic and urban growth with all their accompanying pressures have not invariably resulted in increasing criminality." Based on a review of much recent historical research Thome (1992: 218) also concludes that the assumed causal chain linking urbanisation with disintegration and higher crime can not be maintained on the basis of the present state of knowledge.

The *theory of the civilizing process* as applied to long-term developments in crime is well suited to explain the prevailing pattern of declining homicide rates from the second half of the 19th century until the mid 20th century. It may also be argued that general decreases in property crimes and total crime rates between c.1850 and the mid 20th century support the theory of the civilizing process. The evolutionary trend implied in this theoretical approach leads into serious difficulties, however, if one wants to explain the dramatic increases of overall crime rates since the 1950s to the present as well as the somewhat less marked increases of homicide rates since the mid 1960s. From the perspective of the theory of the civilizing process this leads to the question whether the 1960s mark a fundamental reversal of the evolutionary trend assumed by Elias. Ted Gurr (1981) has tried to reconcile the theory of the civilizing process with more recent patterns of violent crime trends by arguing that the recent upturn should be regarded as simply the latest and best-documented deviation from an underlying trend towards a more humanistic society. Taking little account of recent developments Chesnais (1992) even argues that real violence is still decreasing and only the sense of insecurity has recently been rising.

4.   Capitalism and the political economy of self-control: A non-linear model of the relationship between changing socio-economic structures and crime

The discussion so far is puzzling: *Criminological modernisation theory* expects crime rates to increase parallel to industrialisation and urbanisation. But crime rates have remained stable or have even declined in some periods of rapid economic growth and urbanisation, most notably so between the mid 19th century and the 1930s. *Opportunity theory*, too, expects crimes to increase as valuable goods become more widely available. But property crime rates have not gone up as levels of production and amount of consumer goods increased during the 19th and the early 20th century. The theory of the civilizing process expects at least violent crime to decrease as the modernisation process proceeds. But national trends of homicide rates only partly fit the expected pattern and the general increases of both violent and property crimes since – at last – the early 1960s remain unexplained.

This rather complex pattern has led some authors to draw conclusions which may be termed the "No-effect-of-socio-economic-structures"-hypothesis. Thus von Hofer (1991) concludes a discussion of long-term homicide rates in Sweden by saying that "the profound social transformations of the modern era – the metamorphosis of Sweden from an agricultural to a (post)industrial society, from a poor to a rich country, from an aristocracy to a democracy, from rural to urban lifestyles, an so on – do not seem to have made an impact on reported homicide rates". Similarly Gurr (1981) has stated that "the correlational studies of twentieth-century crime trends suggest that socio-economic change is an underlying but indirect source of variation in violent crime. The dynamics differ so greatly from one period, place, and social group to another, however, that we must conclude that contextual and intervening variables determine the specific effects of change" (Gurr, 1981: 332).

I do not fully agree with these conclusions. But definitely the discussion so far has shown that simple trend models assuming linear relationships between socio-economic modernisation and crime are deficient in explaining long-term trends and their changes in direction over the last 150 years. A potential theoretical model should at least be able to explain why both property crimes and violent crimes have declined for about a century, why a turning point occurred between the 1920s and the 1950s and why an increasing trend predominates since the late 1950s. In this section I will *tentatively* develop a theoretical model that explains long-term changes in crime rates as the result of differing gaps between the normal levels of self-control required in a given socio-economic structure and the ability of social structures to produce the required levels of self-control. I elaborate.

Crime causation at an individual level

The basic problem for any theory of long-term changes in levels of crime is the question what underlying assumptions are made as concerns crime causation on an individual level. Given the absence of respective data for historical periods such theoretical assumptions must be made on the basis of findings based on recent research. My starting point will be "self-control" as a general individual level theory of crime causation (Elias, 1976; Gottfredson und Hirschi, 1990; Wilson und Herrnstein, 1985). I define self-control as a personal *resource* for steering action including an *emotional component* (to be in control of ones emotions) a *strategic component* (to be able to reflexively cope with problems and challenges) and a *normative component* (to be able to act according to internalised moral rules even in the presence of incentives not to do so). All three components of self-control have variously been shown to be linked to delinquency (e.g. Caspi, et al., 1994; Farrington, 1994; Gottfredson und Hirschi, 1990; Kaiser, 1989: 242; Kerschke-Risch, 1993; Miller, 1958; Wahl, 1989). Self-control is both an enabling and restraining personal resource in everyday life (Giddens, 1988). It mediates between the everyday chain of situations and the dispositions of an actor, with self-esteem (Kaplan, et al., 1986) arising as a consequence of successful use of self-control in situations.

The chance that a person conforms with existing norms depends on the interplay between mode and level of self-control expected in a given situation and the mode and level of self-control an individual "possesses" as a resource. While the notion of "level of self control" implies a simple linear scale the notion of "mode of self-control" implies that there may be qualitatively different types of self-control expected in different societies. Crimes occur when individuals find themselves in situations which require higher levels or different modes of self-control than the individual possesses as a resource steering his actions.

Socio-economic structures and self-control

The next step concerns the question of how self-control may be linked to broader socio-economic structures. I just argued, that the notion of self-control entails a duality in that on the one side there exist social expectations regarding "normal" levels and modes of self-control and on the other side there are different resources of self-control within an individual actor. While expectations may be seen as the "demand-side" of self-control, dispositions may be regarded as the "supply-side" of self-control. Both may be assumed to be influenced by socio-economic structures (see figure 10).

Figure 10　　　*Self control as a resource both produced and consumed in modern societies.*

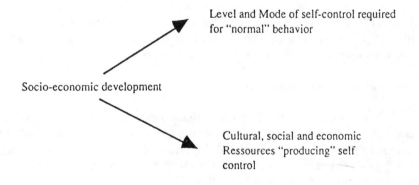

Level and Mode of self-control required for "normal" behavior

Socio-economic development

Cultural, social and economic Ressources "producing" self control

Regarding the "demand-side" we have already seen in the discussion of the theory of the civilizing process that the level and mode of self-control required for socially adequate action vary by type and structure of a society. There are a number of general patterns along which expected self-control may be assumed to vary along with differences in socio-economic structures. Together with Durkheim (1988) and

35

Elias (1976) one may assume that societies with a *high degree of functional differentiation* require higher levels of self-control and a mode of self-control that abstracts from personal knowledge. Together with Simmel (1903) and Wirth (1938) one may assume that *anonymous urban contexts* require more self-control than rural contexts. Following research on work places I assume that skilled work requires more self-control than unskilled work and that work primarily based on communication requires more reflexive modes of self-control than work based on manual skills (Bell, 1973; Kohn und Slomszcynski, 1990). Following Berger (1986) and Buchmann (1989) I assume that societies with a greater *variety of life-courses and life-styles* based on less ascribed types of social status require more elaborate modes of self-control than societies with rather standardised life-courses and life-styles with more closed structures of inequality. Generally modernisation and the expansion of capitalism have resulted in a growing level and an increasing complexity of required self-control.

Regarding the "supply side", self-control could be regarded as a socially produced resource or "cultural capital" which may be disposable to individuals to different degrees and in varying quality (Bourdieu, 1985; Bourdieu, 1988; Elias, 1976). There are a number of ways in which the production of self-control may be assumed to vary along with the change of socio-economic structures. More highly *integrated social structures* may more successful in socialising the expected modes of self-control than more disintegrated social structures (Ritsert, 1980; Wahl, 1989; Wilson, 1987). Persons or families with more *economic, social and cultural capital* are probably better able to provide children with the self-control needed for successfully coping with choices and situations (Rosenberg, 1965; Rosenberg und Pearlin, 1978). More and better education is usually assumed to result in higher levels of those modes of self-control which are demanded by the labour market (Durkheim, 1963). As a general rule, therefore, I assume that the flexibility and adaptive capacities of modern societies result in the production of levels and types of self control that are congruent with its requirements. However, "supply" and "demand" of self-control are interrelated but partly independent processes. This leads to the basic hypothesis concerning the link between socio-economic change and long-term trends in crime rates.

Socio-economic change and crime rates

The general hypothesis is that crime rates tend to remain stable or even decrease, if the difference between the demand for self-control and the supply of self-control remains small or decreasing and that crime rates tend to go up when there is a growing gap between increasing required levels of self-control and a declining or stable social "production" of self-control (see figure 11).

Figure 11   *The basic model of the gap between socially required levels of self-control and their production*

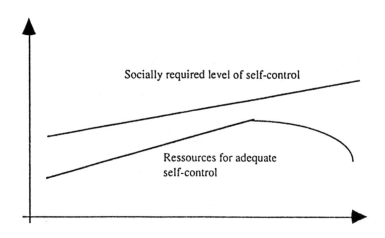

Socially required level of self-control

Ressources for adequate
self-control

How could this model be applied to the two basic trend periods of crime rates as described above?

The decline of crime rates between c.1850 and c.1920

The socio-economic changes following the industrial revolution resulted in the diffusion of emotionally neutralised and role-specific types of social relations that required higher levels and new types of self-control. The *Taylorist organisation of work* in manufacturing and industry, the *contractual character of work-relations*, the *rigorous time-rhythm* of industrial work, strictly *hierarchical authoritarian arrangements in state bureaucracies* and the *requirements of public life in the growing cities,* made self-control based on discipline an elementary personal resource in the 19th century (Weber, 1920).

The crucial question is how 19th century societies succeeded in producing this resource. Wilson and Herrnstein (1985) have pointed to basically religiously motivated (e.g. Sunday schools, temperance movements) social investments in promoting self-control. But they give a very selective list of the institutions involved in the process. In a number of European countries the rise of a working-class culture based on a wide variety of integrating and controlling institutions may have been more important in changing the predominant life-styles and orientations towards self-control in urban working-class areas. Furthermore, the emergence of *politically organising high-ideologies* (e.g., nationalism, socialism, conservatism) and *institutionalised means of interest mediation* may have resulted in more rationalised modes of the articulation of social conflict (Coser, 1956; Simmel, 1972). Finally the *expansion of compulsory schooling* subjected an increasing proportion of children to a highly standardised socialisation in discipline and authoritarian self-control.

The increase of crime rates since c.1950

If one looks at the various efforts do develop periodisations of the process of socio-economic change over the last 200 years, it appears that only one correlates well with the U-shaped pattern of crime trends observed above, namely the distinction between "modernity" and "post-modernity" or "post-industrial society" (see, e.g., Harvey, 1990). This terminology is used in extremely variable ways, but it usually denotes the idea that somewhere between the 1930s and the 1960s a decisive break in the cultural and socio-economic structure of capitalist societies took place usually assumed to have involved – at least – the transition to *disorganised capitalism*, the rise of *consumer society* and *cultural mass production* as well as the *breakdown of some of the myths associated with modernity* (Turner, 1990). This congruence between the periodisation of the transition to postmodernity and the secular change of the direction of crime trends may be a pure coincidence. But there is a number of ways in which the socio-economic changes discussed in the literature on postmodernity, the concept of self-control and findings of criminological research can be theoretically linked.

Consider changes in the modes and levels of self-control required in late-capitalist societies first. Based on arguments highly similar to the work of Daniel Bell on the "Cultural Contradictions of Capitalism", Wilson and Herrnstein (1985: 407–438) argue that levels of self-control have declined dramatically since the 1950s due to ideological influences of, e.g., destructive intellectuals, new educational ideals and a trend towards hedonistic values. Quite to the contrary I assume that the period since the 1950s has been characterised by a fast change of the mode of self-control demanded to become a normal actor and a steep increase in the (cultural, social and economic) resources needed to attain the required level of self-control. Three socio-economic processes are involved in this change: (1) Since the 1950s most Western Societies have experienced a *decline in the manufacturing sector* and a parallel *rise in the service sector*. This process has led to profound changes in the work qualifications needed resulting in more jobs requiring more reflexive modes of self-control (see, e.g., Giddens, 1991) while jobs requiring relatively few cognitive skills have increasingly disappeared during successive waves of rationalisation. The *technological changes* have made high levels of education and the ability to adapt fast to changing educational requirements on the job market a crucial resource for participation in modern societies. (2) The general increase in incomes and the expansion of leisure time have drastically expanded *alternatives of leisure-time activities*. Together with the *decay of class-based regulations of life-styles* this has resulted in an increasing *individualisation of lifestyles* which in turn has made the question of personal preferences a demanding task. (3) At least since the early 1970s an increasing *de-standardisation of both educational and labour-force life-courses* (Berger, 1986) can be observed. While the destandardisation of life-courses may have contributed to a higher degree of social mobility, it also has increased the levels of cultural and social resources needed for a successful transition from childhood to adulthood. Concerning the implications of this process for criminality, Mauger (1991) has argued that young adults increasingly find themselves in a prolonged period of "indetermination" which can result in increased strains as concerns the process of identity formation.

Increasing requirements for adequate levels of self-control since the 1950s, however, have only been accompanied by a corresponding increase in the production of self-control abilities. Among the processes involved in the declining ability of modern Western societies to produce adequate levels of self-control, three are of specific interest here. (1) Since the 1920s a growing rupture between the sphere of work and the hedonistic ideals promoted by mass-communication and advertisement can be observed. While the 19th century may be said to have been characterised by a high congruence of the cultural sphere with the economic sphere the advent of mass-consumption and mass-communication has not resulted in the production of motivational support for the type of self-control required in present societies. Quite to the contrary, the cultural codes communicated to juveniles are dominated by the twin notions of easy access to goods and easy access to fun and action (Schulze, 1993). Regarding crime it is quite impressive that a number of qualitative studies on the subjective motivations for delinquency among juveniles have shown that "action" is probably the most often used term used in self-descriptions of the motivations of young delinquents (Burgherr, et al., 1993; Dubet und Lapeyronnie, 1992; Wendt, 1993). We find that there has been a decline of socially integrating networks on both private levels (family) and social levels (e.g., class-based lifestyles).

Both may be assumed to be a result of an accelerated process of individualisation. On a micro level the process of individualisation manifeste itself in increasing divorce rates and the partial dissolution of the socialising institution "family" in some segments of modern society (see, e.g. Wilson, 1987). The specific problem associated with the weakening of family structures is that so far nothing else has turned up that might replace them as a functional equivalent for processes of socialisation. Both the transition to more elaborate styles of child rearing (including more possibilities of self-expression) and the expansion of formal education, however, may be seen as social responses to the changed nature of self-control required in a late-capitalist society, but they only reached a limited part of modern societies producing increasing inequalities not necessarily in economic terms but as regards the social and cultural capital required in the decades following the 1950s (Wahl, 1989; Wahl, 1990). On a macro-level the decline of a *socially integrating working-class culture* and its institutions since the 1950s has not resulted in any equivalent structures providing socialisation and control of juveniles to a similar degree. As a consequence, urban lower-class areas have been transformed into socially disorganised, culturally fragmented, politically irrelevant and ecologically marginalised regions ridden by growing problems with crime and illegal drugs (Dubet und Lapeyronnie, 1992; Dubet und Lapeyronnie, 1994; Eisenberg und Gronemeyer, 1993). (3) Since at least the 1970s social scientists diagnose a process of growing marginalisation of a considerable segment of European society. Lash and Urry (1987), in particular, have argued that since the 1960s modern societies have experienced a transition from "organised capitalism" to "disorganised capitalism". They characterise "disorganised capitalism" by the growth of world markets, the emergence of a service class and a declining working class, a decline of employment in extractive and manufacturing industries, diminution of class politics as well as increased cultural fragmentation and pluralism. Jan Taylor (1994) has argued that the rise of crime rates in Britain may at least partly be a consequence of the restructuring of its political economy which started already in the late 1950s. Drawing on analyses of changing economic structure in modern societies by Braverman, Piore and Sabel and Urry and Scott he argues that from the 1960s onwards labour-saving technological innovations in the manufacturing sector and the partial export of low-skill workplaces into the semi-periphery of the world-economy resulted in a deindustrialisation of both the US and Europe with a tremendous rise of de-skilled unemployed workers in most European countries from the 1970s onwards being one of its consequences. An increasing part of the population found itself in insecure market positions and insecure life chances. In France Dubet and Lapeyronnie (1992; 1994) have argued that juvenile crime and especially the rise of urban violent crime has to be considered as a consequence of such durable social marginalisation.

5.   Effects of the economic and political transitions in Eastern European countries

Revolutions resulting in complete transformations of a society's political, social and economic structure are very rare events. When they occur they offer tremendous possibilities for processes of social learning as changes in the functioning principles of a society and their effects become observable within a short time-period.

Given that crime has increased fast in Eastern European countries since the installation of pluralistic political and capitalist economical structures (see, e.g., Bienkowska, 1991; Gönczöl, 1993; Sessar, 1993), a number of empirical and theoretical questions arise. Are the increases in crime only of a temporary nature that will come to a halt after – and if – these societies have restabilised? Will crime decrease after the economic crisis is overcome or is the spread of crime, personal violence and drug related problems an inevitable cost associated with an open society at the end of the 20th century? What will be the effects of alternative economic and social policies? What can be learned from the development of crime in Western societies and – vice-versa – what lessons do the experiences in Eastern Europe tell as far as crime in older market societies is concerned?

I will tentatively address some of these questions by relating them to the theoretical argument developed above. The basic hypothesis resulting from the model proposed here is that the revolutionary transformation of the economic and social structures in Eastern European countries has resulted in a complete reversal of the mode and level of self-control required for socially adequate action and in a partial destruction of the resources enabling juveniles to adapt to those changes. With the transition to market-economies, most Eastern European countries are approaching a socio-economic and cultural structure whose main elements are highly similar to those prevailing in Western Europe. There is also developing a two-thirds society with many profiting from the beginning economic recovery and some becoming permanently marginalised. There will also be an increasing influence of advertisement and mass-communication producing strains in juveniles and young adults between the wish to acquire much and limited chances to realise their wishes. Previously existing structures of social control and integration are likely to become weakened without much innovative structures to replace them being in sight. In short: Eastern European countries join the world of capitalism in a period which is characterised by a shortage of socio-economic and cultural structures that produce its motivational fundaments. These processes should already have resulted in a fast increase of crime during and after the transition to market-economic principles. The theoretical approach outlines above would also result in the hypothesis that crime rates will not come down as the economic recovery gains momentum but will continue to increase.

In order to assess these assumptions it would be extremely important to dispose of reliable data on pre-revolution crime rates. However, this task is impeded by the fact that for ideological reasons many statistics – including crime statistics – in the former state-socialist countries were severely manipulated to a degree that is quite difficult to estimate and that may have differed a lot between countries. In former Eastern Germany, such strategies artificially produced crime rates up to 10 times lower than those shown in Western European Crime Statistics. Data presented by Sessar (Sessar, 1993) suggest, e.g., that probably some 50 percent of offences reported to the police in Eastern Germany were not included in published crime statistics. However, even after correcting for such distortions the impression remains that overall crime rates may have been considerably lower in the former state-socialist countries. One indicator that does not seem to have been grossly manipulated is homicide rates (although, e.g., Eastern Germany never reported homicide rates to the WHO). Putting the information available for six Eastern European countries since the late 1970s together one finds the development presented in figure 12. It is noteworthy that the average level of recorded homicide rates In Eastern European countries before the democratic revolutions was already higher than the respective levels in most western European countries. However, until 1989 the data show a quite constant level of homicide rates followed by steep increases in the two years following the revolutions which amount to between 15 and 65 percent.

Figure 12   *Homicide rates in six Eastern European countries, 1979–1991*

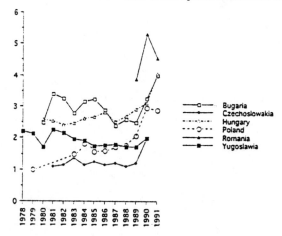

Sources: Vital Statistics, WHO-Yearbook, various years

Conclusions

In this paper I discussed three major theoretical models that relate to long-term trends in crime rates to long processes of socio-economic change. Based on a discussion of empirical evidences concerning trends in both property and violent crime rates among a number of Western European countries, the U-shaped pattern with generally declining crime rates from c.1840 to somewhere between the 1920s and the 1950s and increasing crime rates in the subsequent period already found by Gurr could be confirmed. This trend pattern of crime rates cuts through most of what is considered to be fundamental structural changes in the socio-economic structure of European societies. It is basically unaffected by linear trends such as increasing productivity and wealth but it also appears to be little influenced by the recurring deep economic crises (e.g. of the 1870s, the 1930s and the 1970s). I therefore propose a theoretical approach in which changing socio-economic structures have a non-linear effect on self-control and crime. I extend the concept of self-control as used in much criminological literature in assuming that it should be considered as a socially produced basic resource that enables persons to act with a higher degree of rationality. Levels and modes of self-control required at a given historical period are assumed to be subject to changes of the socio-economic structure. I therefore interpret increasing crime rates since – at last – the 1950s as a manifestation of an increasing gap between higher requirements as concerns the self-steering capabilities of actors and a declining ability of modern societies to produce the resources on which self-control is based.

Applying this concept to Eastern European countries I assume that the increases of crime rates do not simply reflect the economic deteriorations following the revolutions in 1989 but a more fundamental break between the motivational requirements characteristic for "post-industrial" societies and the predominating patterns of cultural codes socialised.

NOTES

1   Considering the growth of life-expectancies over the last two centuries, homicide rates based on total population figures yield under-estimations of increases, given the high proportion of persons aged 20–40 among victims.

2   Conviction rates have increased much faster than victim rates. This is most probably due to an increasing proportion of attempted homicides in the conviction data.

3   Personal communication by Dario Melossi.

4   The decline of infanticides started long before modern contraceptives were available.

5   For some periods data were available only at 10-year intervals. I assumed rates to have remained constant for the corresponding 5-year intervals.

BIBLIOGRAPHY

Archer, D. und R. Gardner (1984). Violence and Crime in Cross-National Perspective, New Haven: University Press.

Aron, R. (1962). Dix-huit Leçons sur la Société Industrielle, Paris: Gallimard.

Beattie, J. M. (1974). "The Pattern of Crime in England 1660–1800", Past & Present, 62, 47–95.

Becker, M. (1976). "Changing Pattern of Violence and Justice in Fourteenth Century Florence", Comprarative Studies in Society and History, 18, 281–296.

Bell, D. (1973). The Coming of Post-Industrial Society: A Venture in Social Forecasting, New York: Basic Books.

Bennett, R. B. (1991). "Routine Activities: A Cross-National Assessment of a Criminological Perspective", Social Forces, 70, 1, 147–163.

Berents, D. A. (1985). Het werk van de vor. Samenleving an criminaliteit in de late middeleeuwen, Zuphen:

Berger, P. A. (1986). Entstrukturierte Klassengesellschaft?, Opladen: Westdeutscher Verlag.

Bienkowska, E. (1991). "Crime in Eastern Europe", in Heidensohn, F. und M. Farrell (Ed.), Crime in Europe, London: Routledge, 43–54.

Bourdieu, P. (1985). Sozialer Raum und "Klasse". La Leçon sur la Leçon. Zwei Vorlesungen, Frankfurt am Main: Suhrkamp.

Bourdieu, P. (1988). Die feinen Unterschiede; Kritik der gesellschaftlichen Urteilskraft, Frankfurt am Main: Suhrkamp.

Buchmann, M. (1989). The Script of Life in Modern Societies: Entry into Adulthood in a Changing World, Chicago: University of Chicago Press.

Burgherr, S., S. Chambre und S. Iranbomy (1993). Jugend und Gewalt; Reportagen und Hintergrundberichte, Luzern: Rex.

Caspi, A., T. E. Moffitt, P. A. Silva, M. S. Loeber, R. F. Krueger und P. S. Schmutte (1994). "Are Some People Crime-Prone? Replications of the Personality-Crime Relationship across Countries, Genders, Races, and Methods", Criminology, 32, 2, 163–196.

Chesnais, J.-C. (1981). Histoire de la Violence en Occident de 1800 à nos jours, Paris: Robert Laffont.

Chesnais, J.-C. (1992). "The History of Violence and Suicide through the Ages", International Social Science Journal, 44, 2, 217–234.

Clinard, M. B. (1964). "The Relation of Urbanisation and Urbanism to Criminal Behavior", in Burgess, E. W. und D. J. Bogue (Ed.), Contributions to Urban Sociology, Chicago: University of Chicago Press.

Clinard, M. B. (1978). Cities with little Crime: The Case of Switzerland, Cambridge: Cambridge University Press.

Clinard, M. B. und D. J. Abbott (1973). Crime in Developing Countries, New York: John Wiley.

Cohen, L. E. (1981). "Modeling Crime Trends: A Criminal Opportunity Perspective", Journal of Research in Crime and Delinquency, 18, 138–164.

Cohen, L. E. und M. Felson (1979). "Social Change and Crime Rate Trends: A Routine Activity Approach", American Sociological Review, 44, August, 588–608.

Coser, L. A. (1956). The Functions of Social Conflict, London: Routlegde&Kegan Paul.

Dubet, F. und D. Lapeyronnie (1992). Les quartiers d'exil, Paris: Editions du Seuil.

Dubet, F. und D. Lapeyronnie (1994). Im Aus der Vorstädte; der Zerfall der demokratischen Gesellschaft, Stuttgart: Klett-Cotta.

Durkheim, E. (1963). L' Education morale, Paris: Presses Universitaires de France.

Durkheim, E. (1983). Der Selbstmord, Frankfurt am Main: Suhrkamp.

Durkheim, E. (1988). Über soziale Arbeitsteilung; Studie über die Organisation höherer Gesellschaften (franz. Erstausgabe 1893), Frankfurt am Main: Suhrkamp.

Durkheim, E. (1991). Die Regeln der soziologischen Methode, Frankfurt am Main: Suhrkamp.

Eisenberg, G. und R. Gronemeyer (1993). Jugend und Gewalt; Der neue Generationenkonflikt oder: Der Zerfall der zivilen Gesellschaft, Reimbek: Rowolt.

Eisner, M. (1992). "Long-Term Fluctuations of Economic Growth and Social Destabilisation", Historical Social Research – Historische Sozialforschung, 17, 4, 70–99.

Eisner, M. (1994). "Gewaltkriminalität und Stadtentwicklung in der Schweiz: ein empirische Überblick", Schweizerische Zeitschrift für Soziologie, 20, 1, 179–204.

Elias, N. (1976). Über den Prozess der Zivilisation; Soziogenetische und psychogenetische Untersuchungen, Frankfurt am Main: Suhrkamp.

Emsley, C. (1994). "The History of Crime and Crime Control Institutions, c.1770–c.1945", in Maguire, M., R. Morgan und R. Reiner (Ed.), The Oxford Handbook of Criminology, Oxford: Clarendon Press, 149–182.

Farrington, D. P. (1994). "Human Development and Criminal Careers", in Maguire, M., R. Morgan und R. Reiner (Ed.), The Oxford Handbook of Criminology, Oxford: Clarendon Press, 511–584.

Felson, M. (1987). "Routine Activities and Crime in the Developing Metropolis", Criminology, 25,

Felson, M. und L. E. Cohen (1980). "Human Ecology and Crime: A Routine Activity Approach", Human Ecology, 8, 4, 389–406.

Field, S. (1990). Trends in Crime and their Interpretation; A Study of recorded crime in post war England and Wales, Home Office.

Flora, P. und e. al. (1983). State, Economy and Society in Western Europe 1815–1975, Frankfurt am Main: Campus.

Franke, H. (1994). "Violent Crime in the Netherlands. A Historical-sociological Analysis", Crime, Law, and Social Change, 20, 1, 73–100.

Gartner, R. (1990). "The Victims of Homicide: A Temporal and Cross-National Comparison", American Sociological Review, 55, 92–106.

Gatrell, V. A. C. (1980). "The Decline of Theft and Violence in Victorian and Edwardian England", in Gatrell, V. A. C., B. Lenman und G. Parker (Ed.), Crime and the Law; The Social Histroy of Crime in Western Europe since 1500, London: Europa Publications, 238–339.

Giddens, A. (1988). Die Konstitution der Gesellschaft; Grundzüge einer Theorie der Strukturierung, Frankfurt am Main: Campus.

Giddens, A. (1991). Modernity and Self Identity, Cambridge: Polity Press.

Gillis, A. R. (1989). "Crime and State Surveillance in Nineteenth-Century France", American Journal of Sociology, 95, 2, 307–341.

Gönczöl, K. (1993). "Anxiety over Crime", The Hungarian Quarterly, 34, 129, 87–99.
Gottfredson, M. T. und T. Hirschi (1990). A General Theory of Crime, Stanford: Stanford University Press.

Gurr, T. R. (1976). Rogues, Rebels and Reformers; A Political History of Urban Crime and Conflict, Beverly Hills: Sage.

Gurr, T. R. (1981). "Historical Trends in Violent Crime: A Critical Review of the Evidence", Crime and Justrice. An Annual Review of Research, 3, 295–350.

Gurr, T. R., P. N. Grabosky und R. C. Hula (1977). The Politics of Crime and Conflict; A Comparative History of Four Cities, Beverly Hills: Sage.

Hammer, C. I., jr. (1978). "Patterns of Homicide in a Medieval University Town: Fourteenth-Century Oxford", Past & Present, 78, 3–23.

Hanawalt, B. A. (1976). "Violent Death in Fourteenth- and Early Fifteenth Century England", Comparative Studies in Society and History, 18, 297–320.

Harvey, D. (1990). The Condition of Postmodernity; An Enquiry into the Origins of Cultural Change, Cambridge (MA): Blackwell.

Henry, P. (1984). Crime, Justice et Société dans la principauté de Neuchâtel au 17ème siècle (1707-1806), Neuchâtel: Editions de la Baconnière.

Hindelang, M., T. Hirschi und J. Weis (1981). Measuring Delinquency, Beverly Hills: Sage.

Hindelang, M. J., M. R. Gottfredson und J. Garofalo (1978). Victims of Personal Crime: An Empirical Foundation for a Theory of Personal Victimisation, Cambridge (Mass.): Ballinger.

Johnson, E. A. (1990). "Urban-Rural Differences in late Nineteenth- and early Twentieth-Century German Criminality", Social Science History,

Johnson, E. A. und V. E. McHale (1980). "Socio-economic aspects of the delinquency rate in imperial Germany", Journal of Social History, 13, 384–402.

Junger-Tas, J. (1991). "Nature and Evolution of the Criminality of Young Adults", in Council of Europe. (Ed.), Tenth Criminological Colloquium on Young Adult Offenders and Crime Policy, Strasbourg: Council of Europe.

Kaiser, G. (1989). Kriminologie; Eine Einführung in die Grundlagen, Heidelberg: UTB.

Kaplan, H. B., S. S. Martin und R. J. Johnson (1986). "Self-Rejection and the Explanation of Deviance: Specification of the Structure among Latent Constructs", American Journal of Sociology, 92, 2, 384–411.

Kerschke-Risch, P. (1993). Gelegenheit macht Diebe – doch Frauen klauen auch; Massenkriminalität bei Frauen und Männern, Opladen: Westdeutscher Verlag.

Killias, M. (1991). Précis de Criminologie, Berne: Stämpfli.

Killias, M. und G. Riva (1984). "Crime et insécurité: un phénomène urbain?", Revue internationale de criminologie et de police technique, 37, 2, 165–180.

Kohn, M. L. und K. M. Slomszcynski (1990). Social Structure and Self-Direction; A Comparative Analysis of the United States and Poland, Cambridge: Basil Blackwell.

47

LaFree, G. und E. L. Kick (1983). Cross-National Effects of Developmental, Distributional and Demographic Effects on Crime: A Review and Analysis. (Paper presented at the Annual Meeting of the American Sociological Association in Detroit).

LaFree, G. D. und E. L. Kick (1986). "Cross-National Effects of Development, Distributional and Demographic Variables on Crime: A Review and Analysis", International Annals of Criminology, 24, 213–236.

Lagrange, H. (1993). "La pacification des moeurs à l'épreuve: L'insécurité et les atteintes prédratrices", Déviance et Société, 17, 3, 279–289.

Lash, J. und S. Urry (1987). The End of Organised Capitalism, Oxford: Polity Press. Lerner, D. (1964). The Passing of Traditional Society, New York: Lipset, S. M. (1963). Political Man, Garden City: Anchor.

Lodhi, A. Q. und C. Tilly (1973). "Urbanisation, Crime, and Collective Violence in 19th Century France", American Journal of Sociology, 79, 2, 296–318.

Maguire, M. (1994). "Crime Statistics, Patterns and Trends: Changing Perceptions and their Implications", in Maguire, M., R. Morgan und R. Reiner (Ed.), The Oxford Handbook of Criminology, Oxford: Clarendon Press, 233–291.

Mauger, P. (1991). "Le statut social du jeune adulte (caractéristiques psychologiques et sociales, représentations sociales, problèmes spécifiques des jeunes adultes immigrés)", in Council of Europe (Ed.), Tenth Criminological Colloquium on Young Adult Offenders and Crime Policy, Strasbourg: Council of Europe.

McClintock, F. H. und P.-O. H. Wikström (1990). "Violent Crime in Scotland and Sweden", British Journal of Criminology, 30, 2, 207–227.

McClintock, F. H. und P. O. Wikström (1992). "The Comparative Study of Urban Violence; Criminal Violence in Edinburgh and Stockholm", British Journal of Criminology, 32, 4, 505–520.

McHale, V. E. und E. A. Johnson (1977). "Urbanisation, Industrialisation, and Crime in Imperial Germany: Part II", Social Science History, 1, 2, 210–247.

Melossi, D. M. (1994). "The Effect of Economic Circumstances on the Criminal Justice System", in Europe, C. o. (Ed.), Eleventh Criminological Colloquium on Crime and Economy, Strasbourg: Council of Europe,.

Meyer, J. W. (1980). "The World Polity and the Authority of the Nation-State", in Bergesen, A. (Ed.), Studies of the Modern World System, New York: Academic Press, 109–137.

Miller, W. B. (1958). "Lower Class Culture as a Generating Milieu of Gang Delinquency", Journal of Social Issues, 19, 5–19.

Mitchell, B. R. (1980). European Historical Statistics, 1750–1975, New York: Facts on File.

Niggli, M. (1994). "Rational Choice Theory and Crime Prevention", Studies on Crime and Crime Prevention, 3, 83–103.

Organisation for Economic Co-operation and Development (OECD) (1992). OECD Economic Outlook – Historical Statistics, 1960–1990, Paris: OECD.

Österberg, E. und D. Lindström (1988). Crime and Social Control in Medieval and Early Modern Swedish Towns, Uppsala: Almquivst & Wiksell.

Reiss, A. J. und J. A. Roth (Ed.) (1993). Understanding and Preventing Violence, Washington: National Academy Press.

Ritsert, J. (1980). "Die gesellschaftliche Basis des Selbst", Soziale Welt, 31, 3, 288–310.

Rosenberg, M. (1965). Society and the Adolescent Self-Image, Princeton: Princeton University Press.

Rosenberg, M. und L. I. Pearlin (1978). "Social Class and Self-Esteem among Children and Adults", American Journal of Sociology, 84, 53–77.

Rostow, W. W. (1960). The Stages of Economic Growth, Cambridge: Cambridge University Press.

Rousseaux, X. (1993). "Civilisation des moeurs et/ou déplacement de l'insécurité? la violence à l'épreuve du temps", Déviance et Société, 17, 3, 291–297.

Schulze, G. (1993). Die Erlebnisgesellschaft; Kultursoziologie der Gegenwart, Frankfurt am Main: Campus.

Sessar, K. (1981). Rechtliche und soziale Prozesse einer Definition der Tötungskriminalität, Freiburg im Breisgau: Sessar, K. (1993). "Crime Rate Trends Before and After the End of the German Democratic Republic – Impressions and First Analyses", in Bilsky, W., C. Pfeiffer und P. Wetzels (Ed.), Fear of Crime and Criminal Victimisation, Stuttgart: Ferdinand Enke, 231–244.

Shelley, L. I. (1981). Crime and Modernisation – The Impact of Urbanisation and Industrialisation on Crime, Carbondale/Edwardsville: Southern Illinois University Press.

Shelley, L. I. (1986). "Crime and Modernisation reexamined", Annales internationales de Criminologie, 24, 7–21.

Simmel, G. (1903). "Die Grossstädte und das Geistesleben", in Petermann, T. (Ed.), Die Grossstadt, Dresden:, 187–206.

Simmel, G. (1972). "Der Streit", in Bühl, W. (Ed.), Erste Ausgabe 1908, Konflikt und Konfliktstrategie; Ansätze zu einer soziologischen Konflikttheorie, München:,.

49

So, A. Y. (1990). Social Change and Development; Modernisation, Dependency, and World-System Theories, Newbury Park: Sage.

Stack, S. (1982). "Social Structure and Swedish Crime Rates: A Time Series Analysis", Criminology, 20, 499–513.

Stone, L. (1983). "Interpersonal Violence in English Society, 1300–1980", Past and Present, 101, 22–33.

Storz, R. (1991). "Gewaltkriminalität in der Schweiz", Bewährungshilfe; Fachzeitschrift für Bewährungs-, Gerichts- und Straffälligenhilfe, 38, 1, 22–36.

Taylor, J. (1994). "The Political Economy of Crime", in Maguire, M., R. Morgan und R. Reiner (Ed.), The Oxford Handbook of Criminology, Oxford: Clarendon Press, 469–510.

Thome, H. (1992). "Gesellschaftliche Modernisierung und Kriminalität; Zum Stand der sozialhistorischen Kriminalitätsforschung", Zeitschrift für Soziologie, 21, 3, 212–228.

Turner, B. S. (1990). "Periodisation and Politics in the Postmodern", in Turner, B. S. (Ed.), Theories of Modernity and Postmodernity, London: Sage, 1–13.

van Dijk, J. J. M. (1990). "More Than a Matter of Security: Trends in Crime Prevention in Europe", in Heidensohn, F. und M. Farrell (Ed.), Crime in Europe, London: Routledge, .

van Dijk, J. J. M. (1992). Criminal Victimisation in the Industrialised World; Key Findings of the 1989 and 1992 International Crime Surveys, The Hague: Directorate for Crime Prevention.

van Dijk, J. J. M. (1994a). "On the Macro-Economics of Crime; A test of the Rational-Interactionist Model", in Europe, C. o. (Ed.), Eleventh Criminological Colloquium on "Crime and Economy", Strassburg: (paper to be delivered).

van Dijk, J. J. M. (1994b). "Understanding Crime Rates; On the interactions between Rational Choices of Victims and Offenders", British Journal of Criminology, 34, 2, p xx-yy.

von Hofer, H. (1985). Brott och straff i Sverige; Historisk kriminalstatistik 1750–1984, Stockholm: Urval.

von Hofer, H. (1991). "Homicide in Swedish Statistics 1750–1988", in Snare, A. (Ed.), Criminal Violence in Scandinavia: Selected Topics, Oslo: Norwegian University Press, 30–45.

von Hofer, H. und H. Tham (1989). "General Deterrence in a Longitudinal Perspective. A Swedish Case: Theft, 1841–1985", European Sociological Review, 5, 1.

Wahl, K. (1989). Die Modernisierungsfalle; Gesellschaft, Selbstbewusstsein und Gewalt, Frankfurt am Main: Suhrkamp.

Wahl, K. (1990). Studien über Gewalt in Familien; Gesellschaftliche Erfahrung, Selbstbewusstsein, Gewalttätigkeit, München: Deutsches Jugendinstitut.

Weber, M. (1920). "Die potestantische Ethik und der "Geist" des Kapitalismus", in Weber, M. (Ed.), Gesammelte Aufsätze zur Religionssoziologie, Bd. 1, Tübingen:, 17–206.

Wendt, P. U. (1993). "Hasst Du was, dann bist Du was; Zum gewaltförmigen Verhalten junger Menschen", in Heil, H., M. Perik und P.-U. Wendt (Ed.), Jugend und Gewalt; Über den Umgang mit gewaltbereiten Jugendlichen, Marburg: Schüren, 13–30.

Wikström, P.-O. (1990). "Delinquency and the Urban Structure", in Wikström, P.-O. (Ed.), Crime and Measures against Crime in the City, Stockholm: National Council for Crime Prevention.

Wikström, P.-O. (1992). "Context-specific Trends for Criminal Homicide in Stockholm 1951–1987", Studies on Crime and Crime Prevention,

Wikström, P.-O. H. (1985). Everyday Violence in Contemporary Sweden; Situational and Ecological Aspects, Stockhom: National Council for Crime Prevention.

Wikström, P.-O. H. (1991). Urban Crime, Criminals, and Victims; The Swedish Experience in an Anglo-American Comparative Perspective, New York: Springer.

Wilson, J. Q. und R. J. Herrnstein (1985). Crime and Human Nature; The Definitive Study of the Causes of Crime, New York: Touchstone.

Wilson, W. J. (1987). The truly Disadvantaged: The Inner City, the Underclass, and Public Policy, Chicago: University of Chicago Press.

Wirth, L. (1938). "Urbanism as a Way of Life", American Journal of Sociology, 44, July 1938.

Zehr, H. (1976). Crime and the Development of Modern Society; Patterns of Criminality in 19th Century Germany and France, Totowa: Rowman & Littlefield.

Zvekic, U. (1994). "Development and Crime: An exploratory Study of Yugoslavia", in Weitekamp, E. G. M. und H.-J. Kerner (Ed.), Cross-National Longitudinal Research on Human Development and Criminal Behavior, Amsterdam: Kluwer Academic Publishers, 381–390.

CRIME AND ECONOMY

11th Criminological
Colloquium
(1994)

ECONOMIC CYCLES AND CRIME IN EUROPE

by
Mr S. FIELD
Research and Statistics, Home Office,
(United Kingdom)

INTRODUCTION

This paper describes an empirical study of crime and economic trends in European countries. Previous research has established a strong association between crime and the business cycle in England and Wales. The aim of this paper is to compare crime trends and the business cycle in a number of European countries using the same approach.

BACKGROUND

The idea that crime is partly determined by economic circumstances is one of the perennial themes of criminology. One of the earliest references to the theme was offered by Von Mayr (1867) who showed that property crime tended to be more prevalent in Bavaria during periods when the price of rye (a staple food) was higher.

More recent work has covered the relation between a wide variety of economic factors and crime, but it has given particular attention to poverty, unemployment and inequality. Belknap (1989) offers a recent, and fairly comprehensive review of such research. However the extent of research on the business cycle as such, (necessarily involving time series analysis) as opposed to the more general effects of economic circumstances on crime has been fairly limited. Among relevant time series studies are those by Cook and Zarkin (1985), Cantor and Land (1985), Land and Felson (1976), Danziger and Wheeler (1975) and Wolpin (1978). The findings of these studies have been far from consistent, and many of the studies undertaken a decade or more ago would not pass muster in relation to modern time series techniques. Many of the reported findings may therefore be questioned on methodological grounds.

Theoretical discussion on crime and economic circumstances reflects two basic ideas. First, wealth may cause crime because wealth generates more targets for crime. When people have money they purchase goods such as cars and televisions, all of which represent opportunities for theft. Second, wealth may prevent crime because when people have money in their pockets they have less need to steal. Stealing goods is much harder work than just going out to buy them. So the wealth of the population may both cause and prevent crime.

The double effect of wealth on crime makes theory difficult to test. It can be argued both that an increase in wealth should cause crime to rise, and that it should cause crime to fall. For these reasons cross-sectional studies of wealth and crime are open to an ambiguous interpretation.

Much of the literature simply elaborates one or other of the two strands of thought regarding wealth and crime. For example, under the economic theory of crime developed by Becker (1974) and others, it is argued that potential criminals allocate their time to a mix of legitimate and illegitimate activities depending on the risks and rewards associated with each. Legitimate rewards will depend on wage rates. Illegitimate rewards will depend in part on the goods available to steal. Both wage rates and available goods will depend on the state of the economy.

Long term and short term effects: the role of the business cycle

Recorded crime has risen in almost every European country in the period since the second world war. It seems likely that the growth of the European economy is in some way tied to this development, most obviously in relation to crimes which have grown in line with the number of suitable targets, such as car theft. Testing such hypotheses is difficult, since reliable comparative international data on the growth in actual (as opposed to recorded) crime is elusive in the period before victim surveys.

This paper is concerned with a different issue — the short term effects of the business cycle. While these are far from independent of long term effects, they are likely to be different in nature. In any case, time series data, of the type employed in this study, are a less appropriate tool for exploring long term effects than are cross-sectional data.

THE STUDY OF CRIME AND THE BUSINESS CYCLE
IN ENGLAND AND WALES

A systematic study of crime and the business cycle in England and Wales was published in Field (1990). Field examined the post second world war period in relation to a wide variety of other factors, including not only economic factors, but also criminal justice and other social variables.

His main finding was of a very strong link between the business cycle and most types of crime. Trends in property crime were strongly and inversely associated with the business cycle, as indicated in figure 1.

Figure 1

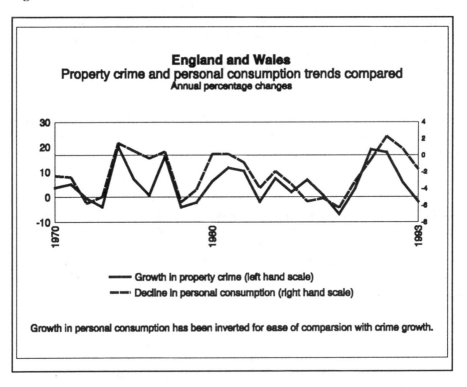

This relationship is apparent in a wide variety of different offences undertaken for gain, including theft, burglary, robbery and fraud. Although it is at its strongest in the last 20 years, it can be traced back to the time of the first world war.

In good years for the economy, when spending is rising fast, property crime tends to rise more slowly or even fall. Conversely, during recessions, when spending is falling, property crime rises rapidly. In good years for the economy, when spending is rising fast, property crime rises slowly, or even falls. Property crime was therefore found to have a counter-cyclic relation to the business cycle.

Although the immediate effect of consumption growth is to hold down property crime, there is a tendency for property crime to 'bounce back' a few years later. There is no long run association between consumption growth and property crime. This can be proved by looking at five year periods: since the beginning of this century, there has been no association at all between the rate of growth of consumption in five year periods and crime growth in the same periods.

Quite the opposite pattern was observed with 'personal' crimes not undertaken for gain — assaults and sexual offences. During favourable periods for the economy, when consumption is growing rapidly, growth in the number of such crimes tends to accelerate. Personal crime therefore has a *pro-cyclic* relation to business cycle in England and Wales. The relation is not nearly as strong as in the case of property crime.

EXPLANATIONS

At the outset, the double effect of wealth on crime was described. Wealth may cause crime because wealth generates more goods available to steal; we might call this the *opportunity* effect. Alternatively, wealth may prevent crime because wealthier people have less need to steal; this may be called the *motivation* effect.

In England and Wales, the immediate effect of an economic recession tends to be an acceleration in property crime. The motivation effect therefore appears to be dominant, at least in the short term. In the longer run it appears to be balanced by the opposing opportunity effect.

There are two possible reasons why the motivation effect is sometimes dominant in the short run. First, effects on motivation occur through a relatively small group — the young males who are responsible for most recorded crime. In practice, the business cycle has a disproportionate impact on the economic circumstances of this group, since they are unlikely to be in settled employment. This means that the effects of the business cycle are amplified.

Second, on the other side, the opportunities for crime are not determined by current purchases of goods, but by the stock of goods available for theft. This will be determined by purchases made in the last few years. For example, the number of cars

59

on the street — all potential targets of theft — is the affected by the economic situation over the last few years; not by the 1994 economic situation. In other words the effect of the economy on the opportunities for crime is delayed.

The result is that the short term effect of consumption growth is to hold down crime, but this is balanced by a longer term, reverse effect.

Finally, there is yet a third effect of consumption on crime. In the last fifteen years the routine activity theory of crime has been developed extensively, stemming from a paper by Cohen and Felson (1979). Central to this theory has been the idea that people are more vulnerable to crime — particularly crimes of violence and sexual offences, when they are away from their homes. We now have a lot of empirical evidence to support this view.

This theory has an economic dimension. People tend to spend less time out and about, whether earning or spending, during economic recessions. Staying at home and watching television is cheap. Staying at home and watching television also tends to reduce the level of crime. This is a third effect of consumption on crime. Although it has some effect on property crime, its strongest effects are felt on violent crime and sexual offences. This routine activity effect almost certainly explains the pro-cyclic relation between personal crime and consumption in England and Wales.

The choice of economic variable

The analysis of data for England and Wales, repeated here using European data, uses personal consumption as the main economic variable for analysis. This approach is unusual, and the theoretical basis deserves explanation.

Under the modern economic theories of consumption (as for example in Ando and Modigliani, 1963) it is argued that current levels of personal consumption are primarily determined by the expected lifetime stream of income and wealth, rather than by current income. The idea behind this is that people do not have to match current consumption to current income. In any one year, they can choose to spend less than their income and save the rest, or borrow in order to spend more than their income. However in the long term people have to limit their spending to that permitted by their lifetime wealth and income. With this constraint in mind, people will limit their current consumption according to their expected income in the long term. A person expecting a legacy may happily run up debts, while someone approaching retirement without a pension may save heavily. It follows that current consumption tends to reflect long term income expectations, and a change in consumption reflects a change in those long term expectations. In a real sense, therefore a change in consumption reflects a much more fundamental reassessment of economic circumstances than does a change in disposable income, which might, for example, reflect adverse circumstances which are known to be temporary.

Although both consumption and unemployment are indicators of the business cycle, the two factors can be distinguished. In England and Wales, Field showed that consumption is far more closely associated with crime trends than is unemployment, and that once the effect of consumption is taken into account, unemployment has no additional power to explain crime trends. To examine whether the same result might apply in other European countries, unemployment data were also examined.

DATA FOR THE EUROPEAN STUDY

Data on crime and economic trends were collected from a number of European countries for comparison with economic data. The main source of data was Interpol crime statistics, but two auxiliary crime data sets were also employed.

Data were extracted form the Interpol publications which collate figures for recorded crime from many different countries from around the world. Data were extracted for as many European countries as possible. Interpol attempt to collect data in categories which are so far as possible common to all the different countries. In practice, the different systems of criminal law, and different means of data collection mean that there are great difficulties in comparing the level of crime in one country with that in another country using the Interpol measure. In the period up to 1976, Interpol published crime data in seven categories and in thirteen categories in the period since 1976. A time series for the whole period was constructed using the crime categories of the early period, associating the crime categories as indicated in table 1.

Table 1:   Interpol Crime Categories

Crime category in period up to 1976	Crime category in period since 1977
Murder	Murder
Sex offences	Sex offences (including rape)
	Rape
	Serious Assault
	Theft (all kinds of theft)
Minor larceny: all other kinds of larceny	Aggravated Theft
	Theft of motor cars
	Other thefts
Major larceny: robbery and burglary	robbery and violent theft
	Breaking and entering
Fraud	Fraud
Counterfeit currency offences	Counterfeit currency offences
Drugs offences	Drug offences
Total number of offences	Total number of offences

Given the large number of gaps in the data, an interpolation procedure was used to estimate data points where one or two years' data were missing. Where one year's data were missing, the crime figures for the year were estimated as being the average of the preceding and the following year. Where two years data were missing, the crime figures were again estimated as being intermediate between the years for which data are available, on the assumption that crime displayed a linear trend during the three years between the two points in time for which data were available.

Finally, inspection of the data revealed that there were nevertheless some breaks in the data series at 1976-77, (when the definitional changes in Interpol data were introduced). Where these were clear, the data were 'spliced', so that the annual growth rate for 1976-77 was treated as the average of the growth rates in 1975-76 and 1977-78.

Applying this approach yielded crime statistics covering a number of types of crime for the following countries:

Austria	Italy
Belgium	Luxembourg
Denmark	Norway
England and Wales	Spain
Finland	Sweden
France	The Netherlands
Greece	West Germany

It was decided to abandon data for Luxembourg, since they are too patchy for a sensible analysis. Data were analysed for the other 13 countries.

Recording and reporting

This study is based on crimes recorded by the police; many crimes, however, are not reported, and some reported crimes are not recorded. Figures for recorded crime therefore measure reporting and recording practices as well as actual crime. This raises the question of the extent to which trends in recorded crime reflect trends in recording and reporting rather than trends in actual crime.

While no direct evidence on this point was assessed across European countries, there are some reassuring points. The evidence from the United States, where a reasonably long time series of victim surveys is available, is that annual changes in crime rates are reasonably well correlated as between victim surveys and recorded crime. The link between reported crime the economic cycle in England and Wales does not seem to be an artefact of reporting and recording practice, for the link was at its strongest in well-reported crimes such as car theft, and average theft loss data yielded no evidence of a business cycle effect on the propensity to report smaller losses. This leaves us with some reason to believe that the results of the present study relate to actual, as well as recorded crime trends.

Economic data

Data on personal consumption and on total unemployment were collected for the same time periods for these countries from OECD compendia of economic data (OECD, 1988, 1992, 1993).

METHOD

Most crime rates show a relatively steady long run rate of growth, such that their growth rates do not show a long term tendency to drift in one or other direction although they do fluctuate from year to year. In this respect they are similar to unemployment and consumption data. In the past, a common statistical pitfall in time series analysis was to directly compute the correlation between two variables displaying time trends, report a statistically significant result (which reflected no more than the fact that time trends were common to both variables) and draw the inference that the two factors were causally related.

To avoid this difficulty, time trends were removed from the data before beginning the analysis. This was achieved by analysing the data in terms of the annual percentage growth rates of crime and economic variables, rather than in terms of the level of crime. (It is, of course, also possible for there to be time trends in growth rates, as well as in levels, but inspection of the data yielded little evidence of this phenomenon).

Initially each crime variable was regressed first against a constant and consumption growth and second against a constant plus unemployment growth. Associated with each regression are a set of three 'mis-specification' tests — normality, heteroscedasticity and serial correlation. These tests are designed to ensure that the assumptions on which the regression models is based are valid. The test for normality is also a useful means of testing the stability of the dataset under analysis, since it will identify outliers — anomalous years for the growth of crime which might equally well be attributed to a change in data definitions or collection procedures.

The main regression models were therefore:

$$\Delta Cijt = \beta_o + \beta_1 * \Delta Sjt$$
$$\Delta Cijt = \beta_o + \beta_1 * \Delta Ujt$$

where:

$\Delta Cijt$ is the annual percentage change in the number of crimes of type i in country j in year t.

ΔSjt is the annual percentage change in personal consumption in country j in year t.

ΔUjt is the annual percentage change in the number of unemployed persons in country j in year t.est la variation annuelle en pourcentage du nombre de chômeurs dans le pays j pour l'année t.

β_o and β_1 are coefficients.

Further regressions were then conducted, adding a lagged dependent variable and two additional lags to the economic variable to the regressors, to test for the relevance of lagged effects. Very little additional information of any significance emerged from these additional regressions and they have not been reported here.

Table 2:   **Serious theft, robbery and burglary**

CONSUMPTION	Estimated coefficients and t-ratios		Diagnostic statistics				
	Intercept	Consumption growth	R-squared	Standard error	Normality	Heteroscedasticity	Serial cor-relation
Austria	5.7 (4.0)	-.5 (1.1)	.01	10.7	fail		
Denmark	6.5 (2.1)	.0 (.6)	.00	9.4			
England and Wales	8.4 (1.5)	-1.1 (0.3)	.35	7.2			
France	9.1 (1.9)	-0.3 (0.3)	.03	9.0			fail
Netherlands	13.2 (2.6)	-0.3 (0.7)	.01	9.5			
Sweden (1974-1990)	2.3 (1.7)	-0.4 (0.4)	.07	6.8			

UNEMPLOYMENT	Estimated coefficients and t-ratios		Diagnostic statistics				
	Intercept	unemployment growth	R-squared	Standard error	Normality	Heteroscedasticity	Serial cor-relation
Denmark	6.9 (1.9)	.0 (.0)	.06	9.4			
England and Wales	4.9 (1.7)	.00 (.01)	.01	8.9			
France	6.4 (2.0)	0.3 (0.1)	.15	8.7			
Netherlands	11.6 (2.1)	.1 (0.1)	.04	9.7			
Sweden (1974-1990)	20.1 (10.5)	-0.17 (0.10)	.20	5.7			

Shaded area indicates estimated coefficient significantly different from zero at the .05 level.

The results for serious theft, burglary and robbery are given in table 2. Usable data were only available for 6 countries. Only in the case of England and Wales and France were economic factors found to be relevant.

Table 3   **Minor theft**

CONSUMPTION	Estimated coefficients and t-ratios		Diagnostic statistics				
	Intercept	consumption growth	R-squared	Standard error	Normality	Heterosce dasticity	Serial cor-relation
Denmark	7.1 (2.4)	-0.6 (0.7)	0.02	11.2	fail		
Finland	5.2 (2.9)	0.5 (0.7)	0.02	9.7			
France	8.9 (3.2)	-0.3 (0.5)	0.01	15.4	fail		
West Germany	3.0 (2.3)	-0.5 (0.6)	0.02	6.9	fail		
UNEMPLOYMENT	Estimated coefficients and t-ratios		Diagnostic statistics				
	Intercept	unemploy-ment growth	R-squared	Standard error	Normality	Heterosce dasticity	Serial cor-relation
Denmark	6.4 (2.3)	.0 (.0)	.00	11.7	fail		
Finland	7.1 (2.0)	.0 (.1)	.00	10.0			
France	6.2 (1.7)	0.2 (0.1)	.12	7.3	fail		
West Germany	1.2 (1.5)	.03 (.03)	.03	7.2	fail		

Shaded area indicates estimated coefficient significantly different from zero at the .05 level.

Table 3 gives the results for less serious theft, on which data were available for 5 countries. In no case was there significant evidence that economic factors were affecting the crime rate.

Although tables 2 and 3 yielded few significant associations, some evidence emerges from the overall pattern of results that consumption growth is negatively correlated with the growth of theft offences in most countries. Five out of six countries show negative correlations in the case of serious theft, and three out of four in the case of minor theft.

Table 4   **Fraud**

CONSUMPTION	Estimated coefficients and t-ratios		Diagnostic statistics				
	Intercept	consumption growth	R-squared	Standard error	Normality	Heteroscedasticity	Serial correlation
Belgium (1977-1990)	-0.2 (20.3)	3.6 (8.3)	.02	49.0	fail		
Denmark	3.8 (5.0)	-0.5 (1.5)	.00	22.9			fail
England and Wales	.1 (1.7)	-0.4 (0.3)	.05	8.1			
France	7.6 (3.9)	0.6 (0.6)	.00	18.7	fail		
Greece (1974-1990)	22.3 (10.3)	-7.5 (3.9)	.20	27.2			
Norway	4.7 (2.8)	-1.0 (0.8)	.06	11.3			
West Germany	7.8 (1.5)	-2.1 (0.4)	.45	4.7			

UNEMPLOYMENT	Estimated coefficients and t-ratios		Diagnostic statistics				
	Intercept	unemployment growth	R-squared	Standard error	Normality	Heteroscedasticity	Serial correlation
Belgium (1977-1990)	7.9 (13.9)	-0.4 (1.2)	.01	49.3	fail		
Denmark	3.9 (4.5)	-.07 (.07)	.04	22.8			
England and Wales	4.5 (1.4)	.00 (.01)	.01	7.3			
France	10.3 (4.3)	.00 (0.3)	.00	19.0			
Greece (1974-1990)	5.5 (8.3)	.12 (.34)	.01	30.4			fail
Norway	2.5 (2.5)	.01 (.07)	.04	12.1			
Sweden (1974-1990)	47.0 (28.1)	-0.4 (0.3)	.17	15.3	fail		
West Germany	1.3 (1.1)	.06 (.02)	.20	5.7			

Shaded area indicates estimated coefficient significantly different from zero at the .05 level.

The fraud results, as outlined in table 4 are striking in that no country displayed any association between economic factors and fraud except West Germany, where the association was extraordinarily strong. Once again, despite a general lack of statistical significance at the individual country level, there was some overall tendency for fraud offences, like theft offences, to behave counter-cyclically: five of the seven countries display inverse associations between fraud and consumption growth.

The case of West Germany was so striking that the data were plotted in figure 2.

Figure 2

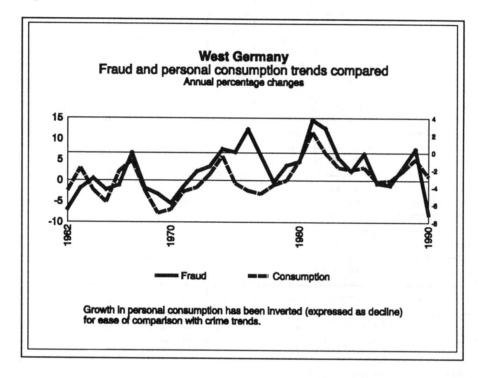

The unemployment regressions are not tabulated here but they show no association with fraud except in the case of West Germany where the association was much less strong than in the case of consumption growth.

Tables 5 and 6 give results for murder and sexual offences. Murder is a particularly relevant crime in that the recorded crime figures may be less subject to the effects of recording and reporting variations than in the case of other offences. No relation with the business cycle emerged in the case of either type of offence, save for sexual offences in England and Wales.

No results were tabulated for drug offences or for counterfeiting, since data from very few countries were adequate for analysis.

Table 5:   Murder

CONSUMPTION	Estimated coefficients and t-ratios		Diagnostic statistic				
	Intercept	consumption growth	R-squared	Standard error	Normality	Heterosce dasticity	Serial cor-relation
Austria	-1.6 (5.4)	1.0 (1.5)	.02	14.3			
Denmark	12.6 (6.2)	-1.2 (1.8)	.02	28.6			fail
England and Wales	3.5 (2.1)	0.1 (0.4)	.01	9.9			
France	4.2 (1.5)	-0.3 (0.2)	.05	7.1			
Greece	14.8 (8.6)	-2.3 (3.2)	.03	22.8			
Netherlands (1962-1983)	7.3 (3.3)	0.6 (0.7)	.03	10.1			
Spain	10.1 (8.6)	-1.1 (1.9)	.01	31.9			
Sweden (1974-1990)	5.6 (2.0)	0.7 (0.5)	.13	8.1			
West Germany	0.7 (2.3)	0.70 (0.66)	.04	7.1			

Shaded area indicates estimated coefficient significantly different from zero at the .05 level.

Table 6:   Sexual offences

CONSUMPTION	Estimated coefficients and t-ratio		Diagnostic statistics				
	Intercept	consumption growth	R-squared	Standard error	Normality	Heterosce dasticity	Serial cor-relation
Denmark	-0.4 (2.9)	-0.7 (0.8)	.02	13.1			fail
England and Wales	-0.2 (0.9)	0.63 (0.16)	0.35	4.1			
France	2.2 (1.0)	-0.13 (0.16)	.03	4.9			
West Germany	0.3 (1.4)	-0.7 (0.4)	.10	4.2			fail
Norway	4.4 (3.2)	-0.4 (0.9)	.01	13.0			
Netherlands	1.8 (1.7)	-0.3 (0.4)	.02	6.0			
Sweden (1974-1990)	4.2 (2.4)	0.3 (0.6)	.02	9.9			

Shaded area indicates estimated coefficient significantly different from zero at the .05 level.

These results provide little evidence of any general association between crime and economic trends. However there were significant difficulties with the data under examination. Some of the data was unusable because of dramatic changes in the level of crime which appear from year to year or because of gaps in the data. It might be that the data set as a whole is flawed by these difficulties. As a cross check on this possibility two further data sets were examined carefully. Additional analysis was therefore conducted on a data set for the 1950-1981 period prepared by Statistics Sweden, and on a second data set prepared for an earlier Council of Europe study covering the offences of wounding, motor vehicle theft and all crimes in France, Germany, England and Wales between 1964 and 1982 (Statistics Sweden, 1983; Council of Europe, 1985).

A full set of regressions was prepared using these data sets. However their results do not yield anything which goes beyond that revealed in the correlation matrices for growth rates, which are reported below in Table 7.

Two main results emerge from this table. First, rape offences in Norway and Sweden appear to rise more rapidly when unemployment falls — so that rape offences have a pro-cyclic relation to the economy This finding is consistent with that for sexual offences in England and Wales, although unemployment rather than personal consumption appears to exert the dominant influence in Scandinavia.

Second, motor vehicle theft has a pro-cyclic relation to the business cycle in West Germany. This is the opposite finding to that reported for England and Wales in the earlier study (which does not quite emerge as significant in the more limited data summarised in the table above).

Of other findings, the results for assaults in Finland can be discounted as a variety of legislative and statistical changes have probably rendered the data unstable. Although the results here show that unemployment, rather than consumption is more closely associated with motor vehicle theft, Field (1990) showed that consumption is the dominant economic factor over a long time period.

Table 7: Correlations between annual percentage changes in recorded crime and in indicators of the business cycle

SCANDINAVIA 1950-1981

		Murder	Rape	Assault	Theft	Robbery
CONSUMPTION	Denmark	-0.31	0.08	-0.38	-0.24	-0.42
	Norway	0.20	0.12	-0.11	-0.15	-0.29
	Sweden	0.14	0.13	0.20	0.15	0.16
	Finland	-0.10	0.19	0.57	0.03	0.26
UNEMPLOYMENT	Denmark	-0.10	0.09	0.15	-0.15	0.04
	Norway	0.14	-0.50	0.09	0.23	0.42
	Sweden	0.02	-0.46	-0.38	0.00	0.14
	Finland	0.11	-0.27	-0.52	0.22	-0.10

FRANCE, WEST GERMANY AND ENGLAND AND WALES, 1964-1982

		Wounding	Motor vehicle theft	Total crimes
CONSUMPTION	France	0.01	0.06	-0.01
	Germany	-0.13	0.57	-0.20
	England and Wales	0.34	-0.28	-0.76
UNEMPLOYMENT	France	0.09	0.14	0.09
	Germany	-0.04	-0.23	0.33
	England and Wales	-0.28	0.50	-0.04

Shaded correlation coefficients are statistically significant at .05 level.

CONCLUSIONS AND DISCUSSION

In Europe, with the notable exception of Britain, the relationship between the business cycle and crime appears weak. Only in isolated contexts, such as in the case of rape in some Scandinavian countries, or fraud and vehicle theft in West Germany, are clear relationships evidence.

At the same time, the results do seem to confirm that crime-business cycle links, where they exist, usually take the form observed most clearly in Britain. Rape in Scandinavia and fraud in West Germany both obey this rule. Moreover, although the individual results were not statistically significant, there does appear some overall tendency for property crime to behave counter-cyclically, as indicated in the negative coefficients on the consumption variables in tables 2-4. This rule, that property crime tends to rise during recessions, while personal crimes including assaults and sexual offences tend to fall has been observed in a number of contexts, and has been remarked on by Bonger (1916) and Radzinowicz (1971).

However the results are surprising in that a very strong and clear relationship in one country has no parallels elsewhere in Europe. This suggests that the driving forces connecting crime to economic trends in England and Wales are distinctive of that country. It would be fruitless to speculate on the answer to such a complex question, which clearly requires further research. Such research would have to examine what elements in the British business cycle are relatively distinctive of that country. One element deserving of examination is the British housing market, which bears a more intimate relationship with the business cycle in Britain than in many other countries.

At the same time, the British results are certainly not unique. Fraud offences in West Germany are very closely tied to the business cycleIt would be intriguing to place these results in a wider international context. There are some indications, noted in Field (1990), that aggregate crime trends in the United States and Japan are also counter-cyclic, (reflecting trends in numerically predominant property crime).

There is no evidence for any association between murder and the business cycle in Europe. This is consistent with results from the U. S. (Cook and Zarkin, 1985). On the theoretical grounds advanced at the outset, there are in fact few reasons to connect murders to the business cycle. Since a large proportion of recorded murders are domestic, they cannot be tied to time away from home in the same way as many recorded assaults.

Finally, the limitations of this exercise deserve to be re-emphasized. It has concerned itself with the short term impact of fluctuations in economic circumstances only. Even where crime trends are independent of the business cycle, it by no means follows that crime is independent of economic circumstances. The longer term effect of economic change deserves separate assessment.

BIBLIOGRAPHY

Ando, A. and Modigliani, F. (1963). 'The 'Life Cycle' hypothesis of saving: aggregate implications and tests' *American Economic Review* vol 53, pp. 55-84.

Becker, G. (1974). 'Crime and punishment: an economic approach' in *Essays in the Economics of Crime and Punishment* New York: National Bureau of Economic Research.

Belknap, J. E. (1989). 'The economics-crime link'.

Bonger, W. (1916). *Criminality and Economic Conditions.* Chicago: Little and Brown.

Cantor, D. and Land, K. C. (1985) 'Unemployment and crime rates in the post-world war II United States: a theoretical and empirical analysis' *American Sociological Review* vol 50, pp. 317 - 332.

Cohen, L. E., and Felson, M. (1979) 'Social change and crime rate trends: a routine activity approach' *American Sociological Review*, vol 44, pp. 588-608.

Cook, P. J. and G. A. Zarkin (1985). 'Crime and the business cycle'. *Journal of Legal Studies* 14: 115-128.

Council of Europe. *Economic Crisis and Crime* (1985). European Committee on Crime Problems. Strasbourg: Council of Europe.

Danziger, S. and D. Wheeler (1975). 'The economics of crime: punishment or income redistribution'. *Review of Social Economy 33, 2: 113-131.*

OECD. (1988, 1992) *Labour Force Statistics.* 1966-1986; 1970-1990. Paris: OECD.
OECD. (1993) *Main Economic Indicators. Historical Statistics: prices, labor and wages.* Paris: OECD.

Orsagh, T. and Witte, A. D. (1981) 'Economic status and crime: implications for offender rehabilitation'. *Journal of Criminal Law and Criminology* vol 72, No. 3, pp. 1055-1071.

Radzinowicz, L. (1971). 'Economic pressures' in Radzinowicz, L. and Wolfgang, M. (Eds.), *Crime and Justice* vol 1, London: Basic Books.

Statistics Sweden. (1983). *Nordic Criminal Statistics.* Stockholm: Statistics Sweden.

Thomas, D. A. (1925). *Social Aspects of the Business Cycle.* London: Routledge.

Wolpin, K. I. (1978). 'An economic analysis of crime and punishment in England and Wales 1894-1967' *Journal of Political Economy* vol. 86, 5, pp. 815-40.

Von Mayr (1867) ''Statistik der gerichtlichen Polizei im Konigreiche Bayern', cited in Mannheim, H. (1965). *Comparative Criminology vol 2.* London: Routledge.

CRIME AND ECONOMY

11th Criminological
Colloquium
(1994)

THE EFFECT OF ECONOMIC CIRCUMSTANCES ON THE CRIMINAL JUSTICE SYSTEM

by
Mr D. MELOSSI
University of Bologna (Italy),
University of California (USA)

This report concerns «the effect of economic circumstances on the criminal justice system».

Based on feasibility and the direction of my own interest and competence, I have decided to focus on the effects of economic circumstances on punishment, and especially imprisonment. I shall pay attention to the role of the courts and the police, but I will do so from the perspective of the destination point of a small number of people who are processed by the criminal justice system, i.e. those who end up in prison.

QUALITY AND QUANTITY OF PUNISHMENT: A FEW NOTES ABOUT MEASUREMENTS OF IMPRISONMENT

A useful way of putting order in this very intricate subject-matter is to distinguish between the «quality» and the «quantity» of punishment. Emile Durkheim in *the* pioneering work in the sociology of punishment (1900) was the first to make this distinction. After him, Pashukanis (1924), Rusche and Kirchheimer (1939), Foucault (1975), Melossi and Pavarini (1977), and Scull (1977), all emphasised the *qualitative* aspect of research on punishment, i.e., in Edwin H. Sutherland's words, the «consistency» between the core cultural values of a given society and «the methods of treatment of criminals» (1939:348). For instance, all these authors noted the relationship between the transition from rural feudalism to industrial capitalism, and the creation of imprisonment — that is the idea of punishing people by placing them in a closed space, organised around the paraphernalia, if not the reality, of work, for a period of time predetermined in advance. In the same vein, Melossi (1980a) and Jankovic (1977) noted the rise of probation in the second half of the twentieth-century as consistent with the transition to a post-industrial society (Bell 1973).

The study of the *quantity* of punishment entails an altogether different type of investigation. Taken the kind, that is the quality, of punishment as a given, the study of its quantity would direct attention to the parabolic trajectory of a certain type of punishment from beginning to end and, within it, to the social variables that impinge on its variations over time or across jurisdictions. Furthermore, one could certainly take the sudden quantitative increase or decrease of a punitive form as a sign of a deeper qualitative change of punishment, as Scull did in the 1970s in his theory of «decarceration» (Scull 1977).

In order to have a sense of the ongoing relationship between forms of penality and the economy, we need instruments to measure both. Measures of the economy are controversial but at least these controversies have a long history. Measures of imprisonment do not yet have such a pedigree.

Usually rates of imprisonment refer either to the number of people in prison on a given day, or to admissions to prison during the year, per 100,000 of the general population. It is quite clear that using either one of these two numerators may make a difference, because the stock number of inmates offers a snapshot of a situation that is the end-process of a long sequence of admissions and releases. Admissions are deemed to be more sensitive to short-run change, but one has to be careful to tease genuine commitments out of movements from one penal institution to another, which in certain penal systems may be quite numerous.

The issue of the quantity of punishment has also something to do with the issue of severity, or mildness, of punishment — even if they are by no means the same thing. We need to tackle this issue briefly in these introductory remarks, even if this issue is obviously tangential to the question of the connection between the economy and imprisonment.

Lately, in his effort to show that the United Kingdom is not the «penal sadist of Europe» (Pease 1994:125), Ken Pease has correctly pointed to the fact that, in order to judge the severity of a penal system, one needs to consider the denominator of imprisonment rates. Pease has defined the use of the 100,000 pop. denominator «useless», because it wouldn't be «saying anything about national differences in 'punitiveness'» (Pease 1994:119), given the very many «filters» that separate the quality of being a member of the general population from that of being a member of the prison population. The point seems to be well-taken. In fact, to consider the number of people who are in prison or admitted to prison, *as if* they «[were] imprisoned at random» (Pease 1994:120) should be considered simply as a starting move, given that the likelihood that an average member of the population will be under lock in a given country in a given year is in fact our *explanandum*. As we will see, every other discussion has to do with complex *theories* about causation of crime, causation of police activity, causation of judicial decisions, causation of actual imprisonment, and so on.

Furthermore, it has been pointed out that the particular mix of offenses likely to lead to imprisonment in a specific jurisdiction might change overtime and/or be different from that of other jurisdictions. Therefore, a higher rate of imprisonment may not mean a greater severity (over time or across jurisdictions) but simply a similar response to different rates of serious crime. This was for instance the reasoning behind James Lynch's comparative analysis of the likelihood that a person arrested for robbery be eventually imprisoned in four different countries (1987). Nuttall and Pease (1994) also show with regard to the United Kingdom that, taking into account the seriousness of the offenses «processed» by the system, the relative usage of imprisonment has been generally declining since the 1950s (even if not for all periods and not for all offenses). This, however, does not solve the typical Durkheimian question: when the composition of crime in one society changes, does the public sensibility about crime stay the same or does it change with it? In other words, will the prevalence of more «serious» crime in a given society make it not lose some of its «seriousness» in the eyes of the public? (Or vice versa acquire it, if «serious» crime has been declining?)

Furthermore, is more serious crime taking place or is its seriousness «better» perceived and reported? There are reasons to think that concepts of «severity» or «leniency» are not confined to the behavior of the courts, but accompany the change of the «public mood» of a country. They would therefore sweep through the public, the police, the courts, the media and public opinion, and so forth. Therefore, the connection between higher arrest rates and higher imprisonment rates rather than mean a similar response to increased crime rates may mean a generalised stiffer stance of society that, in the same way in which it «produces» more imprisonment, so it «produces» a stronger perception of serious crime. It is very unlikely, for instance, that the extremely high incarceration rates in the United States (see below) be *un*related to the skyrocketing investment in policing in that country in the last twenty years (Christie 1993:103-09).

A similar observation may also pertain to the behavior of the public which shows a tendency to «criminalise» and «formalise» complaints that in the past may have stayed within the limits of a purely social interaction or, at most, within an informal interaction among the victim, the offender and the police — as the increased willingness by the public to report crimes to the police seems to suggest (U.S. Department of Justice 1990:5). In other words, it may be hypothesised that the heightened sensibility of the average citizen to «individualisation» in post-industrial society (Beck 1994) leads to an intensification of feelings of self-worth and rights, and therefore to a higher sensitivity to perceived attacks against those goods, and finally to a higher demand for law. Hence, the criminal justice system would appear to be processing less and less «crime» essentially because behavior which was not conceived of as «crime», at least *de facto*, now is.

Finally, it has been pointed out that if «crime» is not the same always and everywhere, «imprisonments» are also not the same, for at least two reasons: first, because the value of one unit of free time (and conversely of imprisonment) cannot be taken to be the same over time and everywhere, and is related to changing economic and cultural valuations; for instance, the value of a unit of time spent in prison seems to have been increasing, at least in Europe until the early 1970s (Christie 1968); second, because a prison system may be more or less severe than another based on a number of parameters, other than the sheer fact of spending time in prison (Pease 1994).

RECENT TRENDS IN IMPRISONMENT

Keeping in mind the provisos mentioned in the previous section, we can make a few descriptive comments about *recent* «trends» in imprisonment rates in Europe. Around 1970, many jurisdictions experienced a low point in imprisonment rates. Afterwards, there has been a rather *general* tendency for imprisonment rates to increase, in England and Wales for instance, and in France, the Netherlands, Spain, Sweden and Switzerland, a result that seems to have been brought about — if any generalisation is possible on this subject-matter — more by longer stays than by an increase in the number of people «processed» by the criminal justice systems. In England and Wales the number of people in prison just about doubled between 1950 and 1990, however Nuttall and Pease warn us that crime rose much more than that, so that it is at least doubtful that the «severity» of the system, if measured on a crime denominator, actually increased (Nuttall and Pease 1994). In France, a long-term trend of decline in the use of imprisonment turned around circa 1970 giving rise to a slow but steady increase in imprisonment rates that the simultaneous increase in alternative measures did nothing to stop (Godefroy and Laffargue 1994). Godefroy and Laffargue also show that a disproportionate contribution to the rising prison demographics is due to the incarceration of aliens and the prosecution of drug-related crimes.

A few other systems have shown instead an increase in the 1970s and then a reduction in the 1980s, such as the Federal Republic of Germany (Graham 1990), Austria, and Italy, where, however, there has been a dramatic increase in the last two years (Pavarini 1994). In terms of number of people processed by the prison system the decrease in Germany goes back to the early 1960s (Albrecht and Spiess 1994). The most recent decrease however started in the early 1980s and seems to have been brought about by fewer short sentences and a tendency to use the tool of formal prosecution more sparingly (Graham 1990). It should be pointed out however that the general trend in German imprisonment rates after World War Two seems to be one of substantial stability and that starting in the early 1970s Germany has witnessed a rather steep increase in the number of people on probation supervision.

Whereas the increases have been generally more pronounced than the decreases, in Europe there has been nothing near the phenomenal increase of imprisonment rates witnessed in the United States, where, with more than one million people in prison and 455 inmates per 100,000 of population in 1990 jail population inclosed, the rates have just about tripled in the last twenty years — after having reached a low point around 1970 — and are now the highest they have ever been in American history and are also the highest in the world, surpassing South Africa (311 per 100,000) and the former Soviet Union (268 per 100,000 in 1989) (Mauer 1992; notice that if one added the more than three million people on probation and parole to those in prisons and jail in the United States one would get to the astonishing count of about one adult American every forty-six being under some kind of penal control!). The prison system of the State of California alone, with less than half the inhabitants of the major European countries, has more than 100,000 inmates, about double those of Great Britain, the former Federal Republic of Germany, or Italy (Melossi 1993:270; Zimring & Hawkins 1994).

Western European countries and Japan in fact trail far behind with 40-100 inmates per 100,000 pop. (in 1991: France 83.9, FRG 78.8, Italy 56, Netherlands 44.4, Spain 91.8, U.K. 92.1; in Eastern Europe: Bulgaria 68.2, Czechoslovakia 75.6, Hungary 146, and Romania 160). What has certainly increased almost everywhere in Europe is the rate of foreigners committed to prison, from about 30 % of the prison population in France (Tournier and Robert 1992) to 15 %-25 % almost everywhere else in continental Western Europe (Italy, Austria, FRG, Netherlands, Spain, etc.), a number that over-represents the foreign population many times over.

Of course, whatever has happened, has happened because of the sum of thousands and thousands of individual decisions made by lawmakers, criminals, police officers, judges, probation and parole boards, and so on. To districate exactly what has happened and why, is the not so easy task of a sociology of punishment.

WHAT AFFECTS IMPRISONMENT?

Whereas Donald Cressey in 1955 could still complain that the contributions to the field of the sociology of punishment were very few (1955), things have certainly changed in the last twenty years, especially after the recent publication of David Garland's *Punishment and Modern Society* (1990). Whereas in this report I would like to keep within the limits of the assigned topic, and analyze the relationship between the economy and imprisonment, I believe that, in order to contextualise this relationship, I should at least mention some of the directions that have been suggested by sociologists of punishment in order to explain *change* in imprisonment rates *in general*. These are: change in crime rates; change in the legal status of specific offenses, such as drug offenses; demographic change; change in the economy; policy change; cultural change; and «self-perpetuation» or «self-regulation» of prison systems. Let us assume that demographic change is already included in the crime rates (Blumstein, Cohen and Miller 1980), and that change in the legal status and levels of prosecution of specific offenses, such as drug offenses, even if certainly remarkable in recent years, in the United States, Italy and France for instance (Zimring and Hawkins 1994; Pavarini 1994; Godefroy and Laffargue 1994), are just particular cases of policy change. We are still left with at least five types of reasons why imprisonment rates may change: crime rates; the economy; penal policies; culture; self-perpetuation or self-regulation of the criminal justice and penal systems. Discussing the relationship between economic conditions and the criminal justice system requires at least a brief consideration of the ways in which the other factors may affect the criminal justice system.

CRIME RATES AND IMPRISONMENT

In the simplest world, change in crime rates would explain all the variance in indicators of the criminal justice system. Therefore, in order to discuss the relationship between the economy and the criminal justice system one would have to discuss the relationship between the economy and crime. Everything else would follow. Unfortunately, things are by no means that simple. On the contrary, there is only scattered evidence that a change in crime rates manifests itself directly in a change in convictions and/or imprisonment rates (Young & Brown 1993:23-33). This applies whether imprisonment (and crime) rates go up or down. For instance, in the United States crime increased in the 1960s and 1970s, when imprisonment rates were stationary or declining. Afterwards, imprisonment rates started soaring whereas crime rates went down and then up again (Savelsberg 1994:917-18; Zimring and Hawkins 1991:124). This may tempt somebody to think that imprisonment followed crime by a lag, because of demographic reasons, but that may apply to the 1970s, not the 1980s, when crime rates went down and then up again. In Germany, on the other hand, crime rates increased constantly between the 1960s and the 1990s but, as we have seen, imprisonment rates went up and down in a rather stationary mode (Savelsberg 1994:916-17). In Italy, crime rates started soaring in the late 1960s, sort of edged down between the late 1970s and early 1980s, then went up steeply again until 1992. The only time when imprisonment rates have seemed «to respond» decisively to crime rate change has been in the upsurge of imprisonment after 1992.

IMPRISONMENT RATES, POLICIES AND «CULTURE»

It seems closer to reality to suggest that the criminal justice system *processes* crime (obviously), but that the pressures experienced by the system in doing so have sources other than, or supplementary to, change in the crime rates. What are these other sources? As mentioned, there are policy changes: these may be changes in the substantive law, in procedures, or simply in the practical implementation of the law. In France, for instance, between the late 1970s and early 1980s, more severe penal practice actually *preceded* more severe legislation (Godefroy and Laffargue 1994). In California, «[t]he explosive growth [of its] prisons was a revolution of practice rather than theory» (Zimring & Hawkins 1994:94), and in West Germany in the 1980s a practice of self-limitation of prosecutorial powers brought a considerable reduction in the prison population (Graham 1990).

It should be noted that such emphasis on practices shifts the attention to the issue of *cultural* and *ideological* change, in the sense that fundamental shifts in the public «sentiment» (Zimring and Hawkins 1991) about penality seem to affect the behavior of the judiciary before they affect legal change — a condition that seems to apply to common law countries as well as civil law countries. Indeed, as Zimring and Hawkins have observed about growth of imprisonment in California, it is «a textbook illustration of the legal realist maxim that there is only a loose association between the law on the statute books and the law in action. The number of persons in confinement can double or triple with no change in the legal framework for criminal justice» (Zimring and Hawkins 1994:92-93). In the German case, both Savelsberg and Graham in separate analyses have pointed to the role played «by a shift in [the] perception of the efficacy and legitimacy of incarceration» (Graham 1990:167) among the German judiciary. An important turning point seems to have been the conference organised by the criminal law section of the German Lawyers' Association in 1983, which focused on the excessive use of remand in custody (Graham 1990:158).

As far as the Italian case is concerned, Pavarini remarks that the rather severe maximum terms for sentencing on the Italian statutory books have never been applied at least since the Republic. On the contrary, a substantial leniency has characterised the Italian prison system with the continuous use of measures of amnesty and indulgence which have contributed to keeping the Italian adult incarceration rate among the lowest on the Continent and the juvenile incarceration rate *the* absolute lowest (Pavarini 1994:49). In the Italian case, a low level of legitimation reached far beyond the institution of imprisonment, to affecting the very essence of «the State» as it is represented by its penal power. This situation is probably the result of a complex web of reasons: contempt for the previous dictatorship, a secular Italian scepticism for rigid precepts of law and morality (Melossi 1994), the political division related to the cold war, and the increasing libertarian sentiment that has developed in the country since the 1960s.

On the contrary, in the United States, as Savelsberg and Melossi illustrate in separate analyses, the increasing rates of imprisonment have been accompanied since the mid-1970s by a deep change of hegemonic thinking in penal and criminological matters away from the ideas of social responsibility and treatment, dominant between the 1930s and 1960s, and towards instead ideas of individual responsibility and punishment, a change that has spread among the public and the politicians as well (Savelsberg 1994; Melossi 1993). Similar developments have been noted for the United Kingdom by Chris Hale (1993).

Finally, according to some theories, imprisonment may be driven by a «growth-industry» type of process, where the increase in size and power of the criminal justice system sets in motion an ever-growing mechanism, as has been the case in the United States in the last twenty years, according to Nils Christie (1993). According to other theories, however, imprisonment is kept in check, in given periods, by self-regulating mechanisms such as those affecting in particular decisions on releases which work as a kind of safety-valve. According to Berk, Messinger, Rauma and Berecochea's study (1983), parole had such function in California from 1907 to 1977. In «socialist» Poland amnesties had a similar function (Greenberg 1980) and I believe that this has been and is the case for Italy too.

In practice it is very difficult to disentangle all these various social influences. They all have some effect on the ways in which the criminal justice system processes crime. And they all have something to do with the economy, and economic change.

IMPRISONMENT RATES AND THE ECONOMY

Probably, the most «classic» statement of the relationship between «social structure«, in particular the economy, and punishment, is Georg Rusche and Otto Kirchheimer's volume *Punishment and Social Structure* (1939), the first publication of the Frankfurt School of Social Research in the United States. According to the original lay-out by Rusche (1933), then revised by Kirchheimer (Melossi 1978, 1980b), changing modes and quantities of punishment depend on the variable nature of the economy and especially of the labor market. This would be based on the basic rule of penology, the principle of «less eligibility», that is the principle by which the prevailing standards of life in prison (or, more generally, of punishment) should be lower («less eligible») than the prevailing standards of life of the lowest strata of the «free» working class — in order to preserve the «better eligibility» of honest work.

Starting in the mid-1970s, there has been a reappraisal of these theorisations. What in Rusche and Kirchheimer's version was «standards of living», has become «quantities of punishment» in analyses that establish a relation between indicators of the economy, such as the unemployment rate or the per capita income, and imprisonment rates. A good summary of the main results of these analyses can be found in an article by Theodore Chiricos and Miriam DeLone (1992), in which they have systematically assessed the results of forty-four empirical studies: «[t]he evidence suggests that independent of the effects of crime, labor surplus is consistently and significantly related to prison population, and to prison admissions when time-series and individual level data are used» (1992:421). Most of these studies were based on American data. In Europe, however, evidence of a correlation between change in the economy and change in imprisonment rates has been shown in studies concerning England and Wales (Box & Hale 1982 and 1985; Hale 1989; Young & Brown 1993), France (Laffargue & Godefroy 1989; Young & Brown 1993), Italy (Melossi 1985a), Switzerland (Killias & Grandjean 1986; Eisner 1987), Germany (Young & Brown 1993), with conflicting results for the Netherlands (Young & Brown 1993; De Haan 1990) and negative ones for Poland in its «socialist» period (Greenberg 1980).

It is particularly important to note the consistency between the European and American results since it is very hard to dismiss them as simply coincidental. We find very ample evidence that change in imprisonment, within one jurisdiction *rather than across jurisdictions* (Young & Brown 1993:35-38), whether measured by stock or flow measures, is strongly correlated to change in the economy, in a number of very different cultures and legal systems.

WHY IS IT SO?

The much more difficult question to answer is of course why this happens. The first thing to notice is that the most obvious candidate, rates of crime, plays only a part and often a minor part in the question. In some analyses crime has no role at all as an intervening variable between change in the economy and change in imprisonment. In other analyses, there is still a definite link between economy and imprisonment, after controlling for crime.

It should be pointed out that in many of the studies analyzed by Chiricos and DeLone (1992), for instance my own study of Italian data (Melossi 1985a), the association between change in the given economic indicator and the imprisonment rate indicator did not show a lag, as one would expect based on an explanation via change in the crime rate, but was instead simultaneous. In the Italian case (1896-1965) the nexus between the economic indicator and imprisonment was simultaneous, whereas there was a statistically significant negative correlation between the economic indicator and the indicator of the crime rate, which lagged by one and two years (Melossi 1989:323-24). This means that, in this case, if there is any causal relationship between the economy, crime, and imprisonment, the impact of the economy on imprisonment would actually *precede* that on crime. This obviously excludes *a fortiori* the role of a general crime rate as the intervening variable between the economy and imprisonment (while confirming instead the most traditional theories on crime which link it to poverty or at least impoverishment). Unfortunately, most studies do not offer a specific break down of the data on crime so, in effect more serious crime, punishable with imprisonment, may very well be mixed with less serious crime, that does not lead to imprisonment. Although this certainly presents a problem, two considerations should be made. First, most studies do offer at least a break down of the general category of more serious crime (e.g. «felonies» for the American studies and «delitti» for the Italian study). It is certainly true however that these comprise many crimes that in the concrete instance are not punished with imprisonment but with probation or a suspended sentence. More importantly, however, as I already pointed out, the economic indicator and the imprisonment indicator are generally linked simultaneously. This excludes *a fortiori* the presence of a crime variable as the intervening variable.

The conclusion that we can draw from these considerations is that, given the rather substantial amount of time that has to pass in every legal system between the commission of a crime and imprisonment in relation to that crime, what we must try to explain is not the association between changing economic indicators and criminal behavior but is instead the association between changing economic indicators and the behavior of society at large, whether of the public or of the official agencies of penal control.

The fact is, we should be considering punishment as an object of sociological analysis independent of crime and criminology (Sutherland 1939:348; Cressey 1955; Melossi 1989; Garland 1990; Savelsberg 1994). What we are dealing with, in fact, are two different social systems, each of which has a different relationship to the economy. It is not a question of explaining the behavior of those who are punished and their relation to the economy. It is rather a question of explaining the behavior of those who punish, and their relation to the economy.

All the explanations heretofore presented, postulate a direct relationship between the economy and imprisonment which relies either on a conspiratorial or an «unintended consequences» argument. On the one hand, the decision to imprison members of the unemployed or the lowest strata of the working class is seen as a way to put a check on the «industrial reserve army» in times of crisis (Jankovic 1977, Chiricos and DeLone 1992). The same decisions however can also be seen as the product of individual assessments by judges with regard to the potential for «danger» of the unemployed offender vis a vis the employed one (Greenberg 1977; Box and Hale 1982). What was still a mere hypothesis in Greenberg and Box and Hale, has become much more than that in Theodore G. Chiricos and William Bales' research on 1,970 criminal defendants arrested in 1982 in two Florida counties. The researchers found in fact that the status of unemployed increased the likelihood of being incarcerated by 3.2 times before trial, and by 2.2 times after having been found guilty, *after controlling for such factors as race, SES, crime seriousness, number of charges, and prior felony arrests* (Chiricos and Bales 1991). They also found, however, that there was an interactive effect of being unemployed and being black, male, young, and charged with violent or public order crimes, that brought the likelihood of incarceration to a factor of 5 or 6, everything else being equal — strengthening therefore the position of those who have stated that «dangerous classes» have come to be defined «by a mix of economic *and* racial, ethnic and national references» (Melossi 1989:317), something which, by the way, seems to be true not only in the United States but in Europe as well, as we shall see.

It should be noted therefore that the connection between unemployment and imprisonment may be the result of more than one mechanism. First of all, the closer to the beginning of the penal proceedings, the stronger the relation seems to be. The association with unemployment tends to be stronger in decisions to incarcerate before trial than after trial, as Chiricos and Bales (1991) showed for the United States, Melossi (1989:322) for Italy, Laffargue and Godefroy (1989) for France and Killias and Grandjean (1986) for Switzerland. Still, why does this happen? Aggregate time-series analyses leave open both possibilities, either that incarcerating decisions are a direct response to the unemployed status of the defendant or, as we shall see, that such decisions respond to a «penal climate» that happens to coincide with situations of higher unemployment. Chiricos and Bales' research seems to direct analysis toward the former hypothesis rather than the latter. However, as Chiricos and Bales themselves note, it may also be that the unemployed condition of the defendant interacts with a situation of diffused moral panic — a panic that is more likely to be activated in the presence of an unemployed (black, male, young, violent, disorderly) defendant. This would be consistent with the findings reported above. In other words, it would be in the initial phase of the trial, when the grounds for custody and not guilt, are discussed, that the authority making the decision to imprison the defendant would be subject to the influence of stereotypes and public opinion to a greater degree (Melossi 1989:322). This type of reasoning may be also framed as a «grounded labelling theory» (Melossi 1985b), as the theoretical hypothesis, i.e., that the likelihood of being labelled would vary not only according to «personal» variables, such as class, race, gender, etc. etc. but also according to the specific historical conjuncture, and the degree of «moral panic» present at that conjuncture. It is such moral panic that we can hypothesise being associated, in complex ways, with the economy.

CYCLICAL MORALITIES

I think that a concept of the cycle is useful in understanding the relationship between economic change and changing rates of imprisonment — even if we are probably dealing with a «long wave» cycle of the kind N.D.Kondratieff (1935) described, rather than a short-term business cycle proper. Kondratieff's are long-term oscillations, with cycles lasting 40-50 years. They are probably more relevant to our purposes, because the force of inertia of cultural institutions is much greater than that of purely economic matters. In any case, the relationship between the economy and imprisonment should not be seen as a direct causal relation in the manner in which some of the theorists mentioned above have tended to see it. Rather, one should connect economic change to the changing moral climate that *usually* accompanies it, assuming that the attitudes developed by participants in the conflicts of economic life are deeply related to more general, historically-specific, social attitudes. As Durkheim had already anticipated (1897), it is at the peak of a cycle where usually conflicts and tensions are higher. This is when labor is able to get a better bargain, and when strike and unionisation statistics are up (Eisner 1987). The attitude in society at large is one of righteous demanding, of lesser concern for the requirements of moral solidarity, especially if such solidarity has to be extended beyond the boundaries of one's class or social circle. This creates a problem for society's elites, because, in this situation, in the same way in which workers show less tolerance for the prerogatives of their managers (whether public or private, it hardly matters), so citizens in general are less inclined to bend to the demands of social authority.

It is in fact in the downswing of a cycle, that the pressure on workers and the general populace is increasingly brought to bear as a reaction against the turmoil of the peak — what I would call a phase of «disciplining», and what politicians often call a phase of «austerity». I claim, in other words, that there is a connection between the *demand of performance* that is placed on a given population at a given point in time, a demand that typically increases in the downswing period, and that principle of *less eligibility* Rusche and Kirchheimer placed at the center of their analysis. *The greater the demand of performance, the lower the standards of living in prison, and the higher the rates of imprisonment.* This should not be understood however as some kind of «State-capitalist» manoeuvre, as it was hypothesised in the 1970s. Rather, it is a moral, cultural, political, and economic movement, a public «mood» (Zimring and Hawkins 1991:175) or «sensibility» (Garland 1990) that slowly achieves social hegemony. The contrary happens in the upswing part of the cycle (Melossi 1985a).

The requests for austerity and discipline that follow the peak of the cycle, whereas they certainly benefit the business world, are not limited to, and maybe are not even necessarily initiated by, the business world. More likely, a public sensibility develops, where the role of (organic) intellectuals, be they writers, preachers, sociologists, legal thinkers, or criminologists, is large indeed. If on the one hand, «disciplining» means cutting costs in production (by introducing a more sophisticated work organisation, cheaper labor, or maybe even moving the plant altogether), on the other hand it means tightening the moral reins on society. The traditional way of doing so is by sending a message through penal repression, for reasons that all great sociologists have pointed out, from Durkheim's (1895) and Erickson's (1966) idea that through public discussion of the law and especially criminal law, communities redesign their moral boundaries, to Mead's (1918) version of scapegoat theory, to Foucault's (1975) analysis of the transformation of subversive «illegalities» into a manageable and useful (for social control) «delinquency».

Furthermore, we know from sociological research on fear of crime and crime perception (Bandini et al. 1991:624-39) that such perception is responsive to all kinds of social variables beyond the «rational» level of perception based on actual crime (social heterogeneity; social change; urban and anonymous surroundings; social disorganisation; age, race and gender of the potential victim; race of the potential offenders; and so on; see Liska and Baccaglini 1983 and 1990; Liska, Lawrence and Sanchirico 1982; Box, Hale and Andrews 1988). Perception of crime, however, is not variable only along such horizontal dimensions but also longitudinally, based on particular situations of moral panic and the consequent amplification of crime. Perception and consequently fear of crime therefore vary with the fear of agitation, unrest, and moral malaise. In the same way in which crime is amplified in a situation of *moral panic,* so a socially described situation of moral crisis — especially if it is described in such terms by the elites who in contemporary societies hold a quasi-monopoly on readily accessible descriptions — will translate into an amplification of crime throughout society and a consequent increase in imprisonment rates. The opposite will happen in a non-crisis situation, in a situation of stability. In such situations, there may be instead a decrease in penal rates.

Moreover, we should realise the implications of taking these public mood swings seriously as a social phenomenon. In reality they apply to every aspect of the «penal question», from the reaction of the public to police reports, from police arrest rates to judicial decisions. When analysts talk about the «severity» of the system, they are not talking only of judicial severity. They are referring to different philosophies of responsibility and punishment, public perceptions of crime, instances of «moral entrepreneurship» with the concurrent creation of new «social problems», long-term shifts in society's attitudes towards the relative seriousness of personal and property crime, statements from governmental bodies and institutions, criminological works, public attitudes on such matters as the death penalty and punishment in general (Zeisel and Gallup 1989; Niemi, Mueller and Smith 1989). One should add politicians' speeches, statutory changes, and changes in the composition and attitudes of members of the police, courts, and prosecuting and defending attorneys' offices. All of these different instances contribute to a changing «vocabulary of punitive motive» (Melossi 1985a) that is undoubtedly associated with imprisonment rates, over time and cross-nationally (Kuhn 1993). What I am suggesting, in just one simple sentence, is that an interaction exists between the economy and what we might call, perhaps a bit too vaguely, «culture». It is this interactive binomial that affects imprisonment rates, rather than the economy per se.

AMERICAN MORALITIES AND PUNISHMENT

Let us consider more specifically the case of the United States. Is the period of «prosperity» usually associated with the Reagan-Bush years an exception to the picture portrayed here, insofar as increasing imprisonment rates did not seem to be accompanied by an especially high rate of unemployment? I would like to address the question by submitting that if instead of focusing only on unemployment, as many researchers have done, we were to pay attention to measures of the pressure experienced by American workers in this period, the picture would appear quite different. Wallace Peterson has pointed out that, from the early 1970s to the early 1990s recession, the American economy went through a «silent depression» (Peterson 1991 and 1994) where, after the «watershed» year of 1973, «*real* weekly earnings dropped [f]rom a 1973 peak of $327.45 in constant (1982-84) dollars [...] to $276.95 during the 1982 recession [....] they continued to fall to $264.76 in 1990. Thus seventeen years after [...] and in spite of the vaunted prosperity of the Reagan years, the real weekly income of a worker in 1990 was 19.1 percent *below* the level reached in 1973!» (Peterson 1991:30).

This abrupt fall in individual earnings was partially made up for through the entry of more and more women into the labor market. The overall result has been that Americans, and especially American women, have been working harder and harder, both individually and as a whole. Juliet B. Schor has documented this increase in working hours since the end of the war and especially since the late 1960s, a situation which has brought American workers, and especially American working women, to work an average of about two months a year longer than their European counterparts (1991:2), and about a month a year more than they would have done some twenty years earlier (Schor 1991:29), and for basically the same amount of money.

One should consider that the 1960s had represented a period of deep and protracted crisis for American society, and especially for the kind of society that American elites believed in. A crisis that was not only economic, insofar as, during the

1960s, profits had been declining and wage differentials had decreased especially in favor of the poor and minorities (Boddy & Crotty 1975:4-5,9). The crisis was also political, social, and cultural, spanning from the civil rights movement to the counterculture, from the student movement to the movement against the war in Vietnam — a scope of problems that was strangely but suggestively caught by one of the conservative protagonists of those years, Spiro Agnew:

> *«When I talk about troublemakers, I'm talking about muggers and criminals in the street, assassins of political leaders, draft evaders and flag burners, campus militants, hecklers and demonstrators against candidates for public office and looters and burners of cities»* (quoted in Braithwaite 1980:198).

«Crime» became a good way to express what was wrong with American society, with the criminals certainly (crime and violent crime in particular went up in the 1960s), but also with work absenteeism, students taking over campuses, pot-smokers, free-sex lovers, rebellious minorities, «liberated» women, and so on and so forth. It was necessary therefore to bring back some measure of discipline and good behavior among these people (who could not find the political force, on the other hand, to build an alternative social model and become therefore the new elites). «Crime» became a master-metaphor to designate what was wrong with American society in the same way in which «punishment», and the connected concept of «individual responsibility», became a master-metaphor of what «the cure» ought to be. In other works (Melossi 1993) I have recalled the many ways in which this sort of penal obsession — a penal obsession that ultimately gave rise to a veritable «crime industry» (Christie 1993) — came to dominate American public life in the 1980s to reach, in the early 1990s, the current tragic follies of the «three-strikes-you-are-out» provisions or the new federal death penalty proposals.

Rusche's theory, once reframed as a theory of the relationship between demand of social performance and penality, seems to fare quite nicely in accounting for what has happened in the United States in the last twenty or so years. Last but not least, such a theory makes sense on a comparative level, shedding light on the fact that, whereas in the United States both the demand of performance and punishment have risen sharply, in Europe or Japan, on the contrary, where punishment rates have increased only slightly or remained stable, the pressure on workers to perform has also not increased as drastically and on such a long period as it has in the United States (Schor 1991).

EUROPEAN MORALITIES AND PUNISHMENT

This certainly does not mean that such pressure has not increased at all, however. Characteristically, British analysts have pointed at developments similar to those in the United States, probably because, under Thatcher's government, the United Kingdom had adopted, at least in part, policies similar to those of so-called «Reaganomics». Peter Townsend has shown that in the United Kingdom, *«on all definitions of income, after making adjustments to standardise household size and composition, the share of income of the poorest fifth of the population has declined since 1979, while the share of the richest fifth of the population has increased sharply [....] At April 1993 prices the average disposable income per person of the poorest 20 per cent of the population [...] was £ 2,926 in 1979 and £ 2,978 in 1990. By contrast the richest 20 per cent increased this annual income per person from L £ 11,126 to £ 18,390 in the same years. This was £ 6,264 more per person, or 65 per cent in real terms»* (Townsend 1993:2-3).

Chris Hale has also shown that the intervening variable between economic pressure and penal policies was the political rhetoric of politicians. He claims that «with the shift from welfarism to the theology of the market came tough talking on crime» (Hale 1993:16) and that the relationship between unemployment and imprisonment in the United Kingdom strengthened after such «tough talk» began.

According to Peter Townsend (1993:3), such «polarisation of living standards» is not just a United Kingdom phenomenon. Besides the case of the United States, it extends also to other parts of Europe (Eurostat 1990 and 1992; EC Economic and Social Committee 1992; Osberg 1991). In France, Godefroy and Laffargue (1994) have stressed that there have been «structural changes» in the labor market that caused «increasing occupational insecurity, a relative deterioration of working conditions and a permanent reserve of the chronically unemployed», and that this is the kind of social change that has deeply affected penal control. They have also stressed the unusually high number of people in prison for cases involving narcotics use or trafficking, and have advanced the hypothesis that with the deregulation of the labor market, and the political crisis of the Welfare State, a bifurcated strategy for the management of marginalised groups developed. Such strategy would focus on both increasingly severe prison sentences (along with the extension of «alternative», i.e. non-custodial sentences), and the social implementation of new arrangements aimed essentially at reducing the cost of labor. This restructuring of government policies has been accompanied — they conclude — by a discourse on «the crisis», referring both to economic problems and feelings of insecurity and popular demand for law and order.

As to the Italian case, I have already mentioned the unprecedented recent increase of imprisonment rates in the last two years, an increase which accompanied the ever-widening and certainly well-deserving judicial campaign against corruption, the so-called *Mani Pulite* (Clean Hands) campaign. However, as Pavarini has noted,

«[T]he extent to which the system of criminal justice and the judicial and police apparatus have achieved legitimacy is unequalled in the history of the Italian Republic. A recent opinion poll [...] shows that the police forces (traditionally as highly feared as they were little respected in Italy) have the support of 88 per cent of the population in their action against organised crime; magistrates were accorded 75 per cent. But this widespread support for repressing the activities of the mafia and corrupt politicians has rendered legitimate a much wider repression. The consensus gained in the struggle

against two great emergencies — political corruption and organised crime — has justified an indiscriminate rise in the levels of punishment. For every mafia criminal sent to jail, a hundred criminal drug addicts are imprisoned; for every corrupt politician lawfully detained, a hundred black immigrants are interned» (Pavarini 1994:59).

The two groups, drug addicts and immigrants, are not cited by Pavarini at random. They are indeed the two groups that in Italy, as in France and, *mutatis mutandis*, in the United States and many other countries, contribute most significantly to the increase in imprisonment rates. It should also be added that this very last recession, which has accompanied the upsurge in imprisonment in 1993 and 1994, has probably been the deepest in the history of the Republic, with the 1993 GNP falling 0.3 per cent, and the purchasing power of Italian families being reduced by 5 per cent in 1993 (see *La Repubblica*, May 13, 1994, p.11).

Germany seems to represent an exception even on the more lenient European landscape (when compared to the United States), since its increasing prosperity after World War Two, accompanied by a slight reduction in inequality levels, at least until the 1980s, was associated with an increasing scepticism about the role of imprisonment, which resulted in a decline in imprisonment rates and an increase in probationary supervision. However, the rise in probation supervision seems to correlate quite nicely with the rise in unemployment during the 1980s (Albrecht and Spiess 1994; Heiland 1983; Glatzer et al. 1992).

CONCLUSIONS: THE PENAL QUESTION AND SOCIAL MARGINALITY IN POST-INDUSTRIAL SOCIETY

This first exploration of the situation in the United States and Europe since the early 1970s, does not seem to contradict my revised reading of Rusche's theory on the macro-sociological relation between the economy and the criminal justice system, and in particular punishment. A certain quantity of punishment seems to be linked, in other words, and independently of other variables, to the demand of performance that is placed by social elites on workers, a linkage that is developed within the public use of moral and legal rhetoric by political, moral, economic and judicial elites. «Crises» tend to be related to the downswing of the cycle and to the need for restoration of order and discipline. These are associated therefore with higher imprisonment rates, as demonstrated in the recent American case. Stability tends instead to be related to the upswing of an economic cycle and to openness toward experimentation and innovation. It tends therefore to be associated with lower imprisonment rates and non-custodial measures, as seen in the recent German case.

In this respect, it is probably useful to focus attention on the emphasis placed by analysts studying many of the penal systems considered, on the very relevant presence of both drug-related criminals and foreign (or national) ethnic minorities in both European and United States prisons. Analysts of the drug issue, especially in the United States, have long emphasised that the issue of drug deviance as a social problem has often been raised by moral entrepreneurs when a new type of outsider, often a «new» ethnic minority, appeared on the scene, threatening the hegemonic moral consensus (Reinarman 1979). For instance, in the second half of last century, in the United States, alcohol was the problem of «the riotous Irish»; cocaine, in its first appearance as a scare-drug circa 1910-1920, of «the coke-crazed Negro»; opium belonged in San Francisco Chinese opium-dens while white workers clamoured outside against the immigration of cheap Chinese labor involved in the construction of California's new rail– and road-ways. The same happened with Mexican peasants in the 1930s, when «refeer madness» first appeared. In the second round of the marijuana scare, in the 1960s, the evil protagonists were instead the long-haired, free-loving, lazy and dirty hippies, white but outcast. The most recent scene has been of course the crack-scare associated with Nancy «just-say-no» Reagan, the «invasion» of crack cocaine (Davis 1990; Levine and Reinarman 1990) that European drug-warriors are eagerly awaiting on European shores. From the very beginning, in other words, identification of a drug and of a human type considered to be an outsider by the hegemonic culture have gone together. Godefroy and Laffargue, therefore, have done well to draw our attention toward this phenomenon in Europe today, hypothesizing that it may be linked once again to deep changes in our social and economic structure.

It has been noted in fact that the increasing social fragmentation of «post-industrial» (Bell 1973) or «risk» society (Beck 1994) has been destroying self-identifications based on traditional concepts of class and politics. Black immigrants in Europe today are, at least in part, a (labor market) result of such changes but are sometimes seen as «the cause». They become therefore the instrument of a typical ideological procedure through which a social recomposition of the white majority is

90

operated symbolically — the social process that found its paradigmatic realisation in the «Willie Horton» campaign of Bush re-election in 1988 and that is still haunting President Clinton's «crime bill» in the United States today. Such vicissitudes seem to validate George Herbert Mead's 1918 dictum:

> *«The criminal does not seriously endanger the structure of society by his destructive activities, and on the other hand he is responsible for a sense of solidarity, aroused among those whose attention would be otherwise centered upon interests quite divergent from those of each other»* (Mead 1918:227).

So, while once-industrial working class, deeply disorganised and fragmented, experiences a demoralisation, a loss of security, values and sense of self-worth and identity, that may certainly result in anomie and crime, the «illegalities» so produced are instantly coopted and put under check as «useful delinquencies» (Foucault 1975), through the work of recomposition of a symbolic moral universe that «criminals» kindly present the established society with.

I would however like to stress once more that these relations should not be conceived in a deterministic manner and that the conceptualisation of a social situation as «critical» or «stable» is what is important and may even contradict the indicators of the economic cycle. Furthermore, whereas this theory can account for variation *within* one country or for cross-national comparisons of *direction of change over time* in *punishment rates, it will never be able to account for cross-national comparisons of punishment rates as such,* because what we might call «propensity to punish» is solidly rooted in a culture — probably in a manner not unrelated to its propensity to produce crimes (Melossi 1994) — or, as Sutherland put it, «the methods of treatment of criminals [...] show a general tendency to be consistent with the culture» (1939:348). So, for instance, the increase in imprisonment rates in the United States since the early 1970s has certainly been extraordinary, however it happened within a country that has been at the forefront of punitive technology and innovation since at least the eighteenth-century, and that even in 1970 showed one of the highest incarceration rates in the world. Conversely, Italy's surge in imprisonment rates in the last two years has been noted precisely because of its exceptionality in a country where «antibodies of resistance to the system of penal repression have long been present» (Pavarini 1994:53) and where «the judicial authorities have constantly applied only the minimum sentences provided by the law, with an almost automatic use of suspended sentences and conditional discharge», not to mention the continuous «generous provisions for amnesty and indulgence (every three years on average), further curbing the levels of penal repression» (Pavarini 1994:50).

Therefore, it seems it would be fair to conclude that economic and more generally political conflict adds but a sort of fine-tuning to the relationship that each national culture entertains with the specific ways it has developed in order to respond to what is perceived as crime within its own boundaries.

BIBLIOGRAPHY

ALBRECHT, Hans-Jörg and Gerhard Spiess, 1994, "Unemployment, labor market and imprisonment: the case of the FRG," Working Paper of the Seminar on Labor Market and Penal Repression, CESDIP, Paris.

BANDINI, Tullio, Uberto Gatti, Maria Ida Marugo and Alfredo Verde, 1991, Criminologia. Il contributo della ricerca alla conoscenza del crimine e della reazione sociale. Milano: Giuffrè.

BECK, Ulrich, 1994, "The Debate on the 'Individualisation Theory' in Today's Sociology in Germany," Soziologie (Special Edition) 3:191-200.

BELL, Daniel, 1973, The Coming of Post-Industrial Society. New York: Basic Books.

BERK, Richard A., Sheldon L. Messinger, David Rauma, and John E. Berecochea, 1983, "Prisons as Self-Regulating Systems: A Comparison of Historical Patterns in California for Male and Female Offenders," Law and Society Review 17:547-86.

BLUMSTEIN, Alfred, Jacqueline Cohen and Harold Miller, 1980, "Demographically Disaggregated Projections of Prison Populations," Journal of Criminal Justice 8:1-26.

BODDY Raford and James Crotty, 1975, "Class Conflict and Macro Policy: The Political Business Cycle," The Review of Radical Political Economics 7:1-19.

BOX, Steven and Chris Hale, 1985, "Unemployment, Imprisonment and Prison Overcrowding," Contemporary Crises 9:209-28., 1982, "Economic Crisis and the Rising Prisoner Population in England and Wales," Crime and Social Justice 17:20-35.

BOX, Steven, Chris Hale and Glen Andrews, 1988, "Explaining Fear of Crime," British Journal of Criminology 28:340-56.

BRAITHWAITE, John, 1980, "The Political Economy of Punishment." Pp.192-208 in E.L.Wheelwright and K.Buckley (Eds.), Essays in the Political Economy of Australian Capitalism. Volume 4. Sydney:Australian & New Zealand Book.

CHIRICOS, Theodore G. and Miriam A. DeLone, 1992, "Labor Surplus and Punishment: A Review and Assessment of Theory and Evidence." Social Problems 39:421-46.

CHIRICOS, Theodore G. and William D. Bales, 1991, "Unemployment and punishment: an empirical assessment," Criminology 29:701-24.

CHRISTIE, Nils, 1993, Crime Control as Industry. London: Routledge.,1968, "Changes in Penal Values," Scandinavian Studies in Criminology 2.

CRESSEY, Donald R., 1955, "Hypotheses in the Sociology of Punishment," Sociology and Social Research 39:394-400.

DAVIS, Mike, 1990, City of Quartz: Excavating the Future in Los Angeles. London: Verso.

DE HAAN, Willem, 1990, The Politics of Redress. Crime Punishment and Penal Abolition. London: Unwin Hyman.

DURKHEIM, Emile, 1930 [1895], The Rules of Sociological Method. New York: Free Press. ,1951 [1897], Suicide. Glencoe: Free Press. ,1969 [1900] "Two Laws of Penal Evolution," Cincinnati Law Review 38:32-60.

EC ECONOMIC AND SOCIAL COMMITTEE, 1992, The Economic and Social Situation of the Community. Economic and Social Consultative Assembly, Brussels, Economic and Social Committee, Division for Information, Publications and Relations with Socio-Economic Groupings.

EISNER, Manuel, 1987, "Cycles of political control: the case of the Canton of Zurich, 1880-1983," European Journal of Political Research 15:167-84.

ERICKSON, Kai, 1966, Wayward Puritans. New York: John Wiley.

EUROSTAT, 1992, 1990, Basic Statistics of the Community. 29th Edition, Luxembourg, Office for Official Publications of the European Community., 1990, Poverty in Figures: Europe in the Early 1980s, Luxembourg.

FOUCAULT, Michel, 1977, [1975], Discipline and Punish. New York: Pantheon.

GARLAND, David, 1990, Punishment and Modern Society. Chicago: The University of Chicago Press.

GLATZER, Wolfgang, Karl Otto Hondrich, Heinz-Herbert Noll, Karin Stiehr, and Barbara Wörndl, 1992, Recent Social Trends in West Germany 1960-1990. Frankfurt: Campus Verlag.

GODEFROY, Thierry and Bernard Laffargue, 1994, "Marché de Travail et Repression Pénale: dualisation et mutation," Paper presented at the XIIIth World Congress of Sociology, Bielefeld, July.

GRAHAM, John, 1990, "Decarceration in the Federal Republic of Germany," British Journal of Criminology 30:150-70.

GREENBERG, David F., 1980, "Penal Sanctions in Poland: A Test of Alternative Models,"Social Problems 28:194-204. ,1977 "The Dynamics of Oscillatory Punishment Processes," The Journal of Criminal Law and Criminology 68:643-651.

HALE, Chris, 1993, Unemployment and Imprisonment: a historically contingent relationship," Paper presented at the American Society of Criminology Meeting, Phoenix, November. ,1989, "Economy, Punishment and Imprisonment," Contemporary Crises 13:327-49.

HEILAND, Hans-Günther, 1983, "Economic Crisis and Crime: National Report on West-Germany." Arbeitspapiere des Forschungsschwerpunktes Soziale Probleme: Kontrolle und Kompensation. Nr.11. Bremen: University of Bremen.

JANKOVIC, Ivan, 1977, "Labor Market and Imprisonment." Crime and Social Justice 8:17-31.

KILLIAS, Martin and Christian Grandjean, 1986, "Chômage et taux d'incarceration:l'exemple de la Suisse de 1890 à 1941," Deviance et Société 10:309-322.

KONDRATIEFF, N. D., 1935, "The Long Waves in Economic Life," Review of Economic Statistics 17:105-15.

KUHN, André, 1993, "Attitudes towards Punishment." Pp.271-88 in A. Alvazzi Del Frate, U. Zvekic, J.J.M. van Dijk (Eds.), Understanding Crime: Experiences of Crime and Crime Control. Rome: UNICRI.

LAFFARGUE, Bernard and Thierry Godefroy, 1989, "Economic Cycles and Punishment: Unemployment and Imprisonment (A time-series study: France, 1920-1985)," Contemporary Crises 13:371-404.

LEVINE, Harry G. and Craig Reinarman, 1990, "Crack in Context: Politics and Media in the
Making of a Drug Scare," Contemporary Drug Problems 16:535:77.

LISKA, Allen E. and William F. Baccaglini, 1990, "Feeling Safe by Comparison: Crime in the newspapers," Social Problems 37:360-74. ,1983, "Fear of Crime." In Encyclopedia of crime and justice. Volume 2 edited by S.H.Kadish. New York: Free Press.

LISKA, Allen E., Joseph J. Lawrence and Andrew Sanchirico, 1982, "Fear of Crime as a Social Fact," Social Forces 60:760-70.

LYNCH, James P., 1987, Imprisonment in Four Countries. Special Report, Bureau of Justice Statistics, U.S. Department of Justice.

MAUER, Marc, 1992, American Behind Bars:One Year Later. Report by The Sentencing Project, Washington D.C.

MEAD, George H., 1964, [1918], "The Psychology of Punitive Justice." Pp.212-39 in G. H. Mead, Selected Writings, Indianapolis: Bobbs-Merrill.

MELOSSI, Dario, 1994, "The 'Economy' of Illegalities: Normal Crimes, Elites and Social Control in Comparative Analysis." Pp.202-19 in D.Nelken (Ed.), The Futures of Criminology. London: SAGE. 1993, "Gazette of Morality and Social Whip: Punishment, Hegemony and the Case of the USA, 1970-92," Social and Legal Studies 2:259-79.

MELOSSI (cont.), 1989, "An Introduction: Fifty Years Later, *Punishment and Social Structure In Comparative Analysis.*" Contemporary Crises 13:311-26.
1985a, "Punishment and Social Action: Changing Vocabularies of Punitive Motive Within A Political Business Cycle," Current Perspectives in Social Theory 6:169-197.
1985b, "Overcoming the Crisis in Critical Criminology: Toward a grounded labeling theory," Criminology 23:193-208.
1980a, "Strategies of Social Control in Capitalism: A comment on recent work," Contemporary Crises 4:381-402.
1980b, "Georg Rusche: A Biographical Essay," Crime and Social Justice 14:51-63.
1978, "Georg Rusche and Otto Kirchheimer: *Punishment and Social Structure,*" Crime and Social Justice 9:73-85.

MELOSSI, Dario and Massimo Pavarini, 1981, [1977], The Prison and the Factory: Origins of the Penitentiary System. London: Macmillan.

NIEMI, Richard G., John Mueller and Tom W. Smith, 1989, Trends in Public Opinion: A Compendium of Survey Data. New York: Greenwood Press.

NUTTALL, Christopher and Ken Pease, 1994, "Changes in the Use of Imprisonment in England and Wales 1950-1991," Criminal Law Review, May, pp.316-23.

OSBERG, L. (Ed.), 1991, Economic Inequality and Poverty: International Perspectives. New York: Sharpe.

PASHUKANIS, Evgeny B., 1980, [1924], "The General Theory of Law and Marxism." Pp.40-131 in E.B.Pashukanis, Selected Writings on Marxism and Law. London: Academic Press.

PAVARINI, Massimo, 1994, "The New Penology and Politics in Crisis: The Italian Case," British Journal of Criminology 34(special issue): 49-61.

PEASE, Ken, 1994, "Cross-National Imprisonment Rates: Limitations of Method and Possible Conclusions," British Journal of Criminology 34 (special issue): 116-30.

PETERSON, Wallace G., 1994, Silent Depression: The Fate of the American Dream. New York: Norton. ,1991, "The Silent Depression," Challenge 34/4:29-34.

REINARMAN, Craig, 1979, "Moral Entrepreneurs and Political Economy: Historical and Ethnographic Notes on the Construction of the Cocaine Menace," Contemporary Crises 3:225-54.

RUSCHE, Georg, 1933, "Labor Market and Penal Sanction," Crime and Social Justice 10:2-8.

RUSCHE, Georg and Otto Kirchheimer, 1968, [1939], Punishment and Social Structure. New York: Russell & Russell.

SAVELSBERG, Joachim J., 1994, "Knowledge, Domination, and Criminal Punishment," American Journal of Sociology 99:911-43.

SCHOR, Juliet B., 1991, The Overworked American. New York: Basic Books.

SCULL, Andrew, 1977, Decarceration: Community Treatment and the Deviant: A Radical View. Englewood Cliffs(NJ): Prentice-Hall.

SUTHERLAND, Edwin H., 1939, Principles of Criminology. Philadelphia: Lippincott.

TOURNIER, Pierre and Philippe Robert, 1992, "Etrangers: police, justice, prison." In Haut Conseil à l'intégration, La connaissance de l'immigration et de l'intégration. Rapport au Premier ministre. Décembre. Paris: La documentation Française.

TOWNSEND, Peter, 1993, "The Repressive Nature and Extent of Poverty in the UK: Predisposing Cause of Crime." Paper presented at the Symposium on "The Link Between Poverty and Crime," Eleventh Annual Conference of the Howard League on "Poverty and Crime," 8-10 September.

UNITED STATES DEPARTMENT OF JUSTICE, 1990, Criminal Victimisation 1989. Statistics Bulletin of the Department of Justice, Bureau of Justice, Washington DC.

YOUNG, Warren and Mark Brown, 1993, "Cross-National Comparisons of Imprisonment." In M. Tonroy (Ed.), Crime and Justice: A Review of Research. Volume 17.

ZEISEL, Hans and Alec M. Gallup, 1989, "Death Penalty Sentiment in the United States," Journal of Quantitative Criminology 5:285-96.

ZIMRING, Franklin E. and Gordon Hawkins, 1994, "The Growth of Imprisonment in California," British Journal of Criminology 34(Special Issue): 83-96. ,1991, The Scale of Imprisonment. Chicago: The University of Chicago Press.

CRIME AND ECONOMY

11th Criminological
Colloquium
(1994)

OPPORTUNITIES FOR CRIME:
A TEST OF THE RATIONAL-INTERACTIONIST MODEL

by
Mr J.M. Van DIJK
Ministry of Justice,
University of Leyden
(The Netherlands)

«Opportunity makes the thief»
«De gelegenheid maakt de dief»
«Gelegenheit macht Diebe»
«L'occasion fait le larron»
«L'ocasión hace al ladrón»
«L'occasione fa l'uomo ladro»

INTRODUCTION[1]

Up to recent years the only generally available measures of crime which criminology had at its disposal were the rates of officially recorded crimes. Differences in rates of recorded crime in time or space were as likely the result of diverging reporting patterns or/and recording practices as of true differences in the volume of crime. Without exception empirical studies of crime as a social phenomenon — so-called macro-criminological studies — were methodologically flawed. The problems were particularly great in the case of international comparisons. In the past decades when more was understood of diverging legal definitions, reporting patterns and recording practices of the police, macro-criminological studies were increasingly discredited (Wilkins, 1980). In spite of this, some theoretically interesting new studies were yet carried out (Schichor, 1990; Bennett, 1991; Herland, Shelley, Katoh, 1992).

In recent years crime levels are in many countries measured independently from the institutions of criminal justice, by means of surveys among the public about personal experiences of crime. The execution of victimisation surveys in a large number of countries opens new perspectives for comparative criminology, if international standards are applied.

In 1987 the initiative was taken to carry out fully standardised surveys in as many countries as possible (Van Dijk, Mayhew, Killias, 1989). To date the ICS was carried out in more than forty countries from all hemispheres (Del Frate, Zvekic, Van Dijk, 1993). The integrated ICS data-set of Leyden University yields credible information on national crime levels and their social correlates of 38 countries. The ICS database presents an unprecedented opportunity for the development and testing of criminological theories at the macro level. In a review of its methodological merits, the International Crime Surveys project was characterised as a «quantum-leap in international statistics on crime and justice issues» (Lynch, 1993).

Comparisons of victimisation rates pose a major theoretical challenge for criminology. Now that credible crime figures become available, modern criminology may break away from its long preoccupation with the personality features of individual offenders. The victimisation studies may foster a renewed interest in the social causes of crime at the macro level in the venerable tradition of Quetelet, Ferri, Lacassagne, Durkheim and Bonger.

Such analyses at the macro level also have great potential for enhancing the policy utility of criminological studies. Comparisons of national victimisation rates are of interest to the media by putting national crime problems in an international perspective. However, for governments whose countries show high crime rates such league tables are often politically embarrassing. To make matters worse league tables by themselves do not provide much understanding of the macro causes of national crime problems and/or of the most promising policies to pursue (Erbès, 1991). In this situation league tables of crime give ample scope for political exploitation and stereotyping of foreign countries.

If differences between national crime rates can to some extent be theoretically explained, this would greatly increase the policy relevance of comparative criminology. Criminologists would be able to both describe and diagnose national crime situations and come forward with grounded advice on the general policies to pursue (Petersilia, 1991; Braithwaite, 1989). In so doing, criminology might be able to outgrow its «adversarial nihilism» (Cohen, 1990) and increase its influence on political decision making.

In this paper we will first present some league tables of national victimisation rates. We will then draw attention to the ambiguous relationship between levels of affluence/modernisation and victimisation/crime rates. We will subsequently present the outlines of a theoretical model — the rational interactionist model — which sheds light on the antagonistic effects of affluence on crime rates. Next the results of a series of multivariate analyses of victimisation rates and other data taken from the ICS will be presented as an empirical test of several hypotheses derived from the model. Finally we will try to interpret the national victimisation rates of 33 countries in the light of the thus tested theoretical perspective and comment upon possible policy implications.

AFFLUENCE AND NATIONAL CRIME RATES

National crime rates

In table 1 is depicted the percentage of the public of industrialised countries victimised by any crime in the last year according to the ICS studies.

Table 1: *Percentage of the public in industrialised countries victimised by any crime during twelve months; results of the ICS 1998 and 1991*

There is no obvious explanation for the ranking of countries according to overall victimisation risks. Of the Western countries the USA, Canada, Australia, New Zealand,the United Kingdom (1991) and the Netherlands show the highest rates. These countries enjoy relatively high levels of affluence. Equally high rates, however, were measured in poorer countries like Spain and some ex-socialist countries, notably Poland and Estonia, whose economies are currently being restructured.

Possibly crime specific victimisation rates show rankings which suggest a straightforward causal interpretation.

Tables 2 to 4 present the national victimisation rates for car theft, burglary and robbery respectively.

Table 2:   *Percentage of the public victimised by car theft over a period of twelve months; results of the ICS 1988 and 1991*

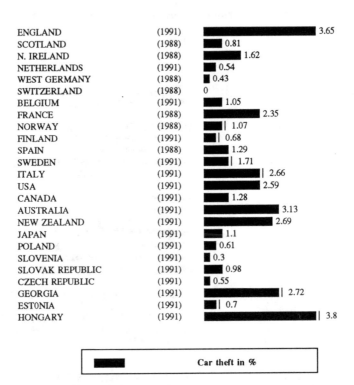

		Car theft in %
ENGLAND	(1991)	3.65
SCOTLAND	(1988)	0.81
N. IRELAND	(1988)	1.62
NETHERLANDS	(1991)	0.54
WEST GERMANY	(1988)	0.43
SWITZERLAND	(1988)	0
BELGIUM	(1991)	1.05
FRANCE	(1988)	2.35
NORWAY	(1988)	1.07
FINLAND	(1991)	0.68
SPAIN	(1988)	1.29
SWEDEN	(1991)	1.71
ITALY	(1991)	2.66
USA	(1991)	2.59
CANADA	(1991)	1.28
AUSTRALIA	(1991)	3.13
NEW ZEALAND	(1991)	2.69
JAPAN	(1991)	1.1
POLAND	(1991)	0.61
SLOVENIA	(1991)	0.3
SLOVAK REPUBLIC	(1991)	0.98
CZECH REPUBLIC	(1991)	0.55
GEORGIA	(1991)	2.72
ESTONIA	(1991)	0.7
HONGARY	(1991)	3.8

The prevalence rates for car theft are highest in relatively affluent countries like the United Kingdom, Italy, Australia, New Zealand, France and the USA. Hungary too shows a surprisingly high rate. The rates are low in some other relatively affluent countries, notably W. Germany, Switzerland, the Netherlands and Finland.

102

Table 3:   *Percentage of the public victimised by burglary over a period of twelve months; results of the ICS 1988 and 1991*

Country	Year	Burglary in %
ENGLAND	(1991)	2.97
SCOTLAND	(1988)	2.03
N. IRELAND	(1988)	1.11
NETHERLANDS	(1991)	1.96
WEST GERMANY	(1988)	1.29
SWITZERLAND	(1988)	0.97
BELGIUM	(1991)	2.11
FRANCE	(1988)	2.37
NORWAY	(1988)	0.75
FINLAND	(1991)	0.62
SPAIN	(1988)	1.72
SWEDEN	(1991)	1.36
ITALY	(1991)	2.39
USA	(1991)	3.14
CANADA	(1991)	3.36
AUSTRALIA	(1991)	3.68
NEW ZEALAND	(1991)	4.3
JAPAN	(1991)	1.1
POLAND	(1991)	2.25
SLOVENIA	(1991)	1.8
SLOVAK REPUBLIC	(1991)	3.35
CZECH REPUBLIC	(1991)	4.68
GEORGIA	(1991)	2.51
ESTONIA	(1991)	5.6
HONGARY	(1991)	1.4

Burglars get into people's homes most frequently in affluent North America and Australia and in the much less affluent Czech Republic and Estonia.

103

Table 4: *Percentage of the public victimised by robbery over a period of twelve months; results of the ICS 1988 and 1991*

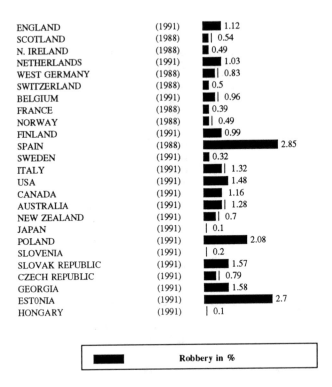

		Robbery in %
ENGLAND	(1991)	1.12
SCOTLAND	(1988)	0.54
N. IRELAND	(1988)	0.49
NETHERLANDS	(1991)	1.03
WEST GERMANY	(1988)	0.83
SWITZERLAND	(1988)	0.5
BELGIUM	(1991)	0.96
FRANCE	(1988)	0.39
NORWAY	(1988)	0.49
FINLAND	(1991)	0.99
SPAIN	(1988)	2.85
SWEDEN	(1991)	0.32
ITALY	(1991)	1.32
USA	(1991)	1.48
CANADA	(1991)	1.16
AUSTRALIA	(1991)	1.28
NEW ZEALAND	(1991)	0.7
JAPAN	(1991)	0.1
POLAND	(1991)	2.08
SLOVENIA	(1991)	0.2
SLOVAK REPUBLIC	(1991)	1.57
CZECH REPUBLIC	(1991)	0.79
GEORGIA	(1991)	1.58
ESTONIA	(1991)	2.7
HONGARY	(1991)	0.1

The one-year victimisation rates for robbery were highest in Estonia, Spain, Poland, the USA and Italy. The rates tend to be higher in less affluent countries but the USA is an exception.

The ranking of countries is different for each type of crime. The crime-specific rates do not show a consistent link between affluence and levels of victimisation either.

URBAN CRIME RATES OF GLOBAL AREAS

The ICS of 1992 was also carried out in the capitals or major cities of some developing countries. Since many developing nations lack national statistical data on crime the ICS has broken new ground here. The results refute the hypothesis of an unilinear relationship between affluence/modernisation and crime. Megacities in Africa, Papua New Guinea and South America show by far the highest rates for most types of property crime. Previous findings indicating a positive link between national levels of affluence and property crimes (Shickor, 1990; Siemanszko, 1992; UN, 1993) were probably an artefact of better incident reporting and police recording in affluent nations.

In order to gain perspective we compared the city rates of developing countries with the rates of inhabitants of cities with more than 100,000 inhabitants in the other countries. Table 5 depicts the rates for car crime (theft of cars, from cars and car vandalism), burglary, contact theft (robbery and violent and sexual crimes), other theft and any crime, disaggregated according to global region.

We have distinguished between the Western European countries (13), East European countries (8), the New World countries (the USA, Canada, Australia and New Zealand), South America (Argentina, Brazil, Costa Rica), Asia (Japan, India, Indonesia, Philippines) and Africa (Tanzania, Uganda, Egypt, South Africa and Tunisia)[2].

Table 5:   *Percentage of the public in large cities (> 100,000 inhabitants) victimised by four types of crime and any crime in the urban areas of six global regions; results of the ICS 1988 and 1991*

	Total	Western Europe	New World	South America	Eastern Europe	Asia	Africa
Total	74 000	28 000	8 000	6 000	14 000	8 000	18 000
Car crime	29.0	33.6	43.3	24.8	26.5	11.8	24.2
Burglary	20.2	16.3	24.0	20.2	17.5	13.0	37.5
Other theft	29.3	27.1	26.0	32.7	27.7	24.6	42.1
Contact crime	19.3	15.3	19.8	31.4	16.9	10.8	33.4
Any crime	**60.7**	**59.8**	**64.6**	**68.4**	**55.8**	**43.9**	**75.7**

The highest overall victimisation rates are found in Africa, South America and the New World. The overall crime rates of Western and East or Central European countries are almost identical, although car crime is more prevalent in the West.

The data show that car crime is more prevalent in the more affluent parts of the world, that is in cities in the New World and Western European countries. Burglary rates are highest in cities in Africa and, again, in the New World. Rates for contact crime are by far highest in Africa and South America. Differences between the rates of other theft are less marked although here also Africa shows the highest rates.

PLOTTING NATIONAL CRIME RATES BY AFFLUENCE

In figure 1 are plotted the overall victimisation rates of city dwellers per country by the average level of affluence (a combined measure of mean educational attainment and national product per capita)[3]. The rates of developing countries, ex-communist European countries, New World countries, including Japan and other European countries are identified with numbers in reversed order (4, 3, 2, 1).

105

Figure 1:   *Overall victimisation rates of urban dwellers in 32 countries by levels of affluence; developing, ex-communist, New World and European countries are depicted with the numbers 4, 3, 2, 1 respectively (ICS 1988 and 1991)*

plot of victim with affluence by country

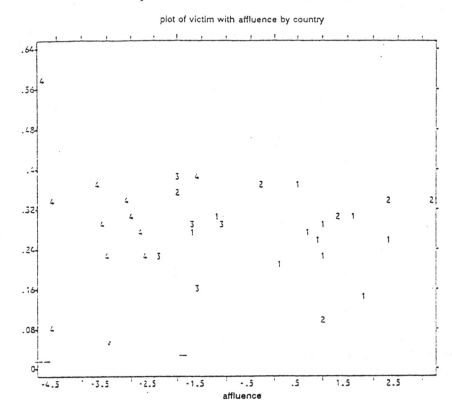

plot of victim with affluence by country

The outliers at the bottom with overall victimisation rates below ten are India (4) and Japan (2). The plot does not show a linear relationship between affluence and national crime rates. Crime in general seems to be a common plight of urban dwellers in poor and rich societies.

These key epidemiological findings of the ICS constitute a theoretical puzzle. Somewhat paradoxically both poverty and affluence seem to breed high levels of crime.

TOWARDS AN INTEGRATED MODEL

According to macro theories of crime in the motivational tradition of Von Mayr, Bonger (1905) and Merton (1957) the level of crime is largely determined by the economical situation of the potential perpetrators. If more people suffer from economic hardship or frustrated economic or social aspirations, more will be ready to commit profitable crimes or increase their rate of offending. Relationships were consistently found between measures of poverty/inequality and recorded crimes of violence (Ching-Chi Hsieh and M.D. Pugh, 1993). However, the research findings on the relationships between poverty/inequality and recorded property crimes are ambiguous (Chiricos, 1987; Belknap, 1989). It follows from strain theory perspective that crime rates must be lower among national populations which enjoy high levels of reasonably well-distributed affluence. The absence of a consistent relationship between affluence and national crime rates cannot be easily reconciled with this theoretical perspective. The indisputable post war boom of most types of crime in the industrialised world also flies in the face of it (Svensson, 1986; Norström, 1988; Van Dijk, 1991). The present high crime rates in affluent and egalitarian welfare-minded societies like Sweden, the Netherlands, Canada and New Zealand in particular seem to refute Bongerian notions of poverty breeding crime. In fact the only country which seems to conform to these notions is affluent, egalitarian and low crime Japan[4].

According to criminal opportunity theory crime rates are determined by the convergence in space and time of motivated offenders and suitable targets, in the absence of sufficient social guardianship. In this alternative perspective of Mayhew et.al. (1976), Cohen and Felson (1979) and Van Dijk and Steinmetz (1979) high levels of affluence lead to higher crime rates through a wider availability of suitable and poorly guarded targets of crime. A larger supply of suitable targets will attract more offenders and allow them to reach a higher frequency of offending. This perspective seems important for the analysis of crime rates in industrialised countries. The strain perspective seems more relevant for the study of crime rates in countries where the supply of targets is limited.

In recent years attempts have been made to develop integrated or synthetic models for analysing crime rates (Balkin and McDonald, 1980; Cook, 1986; Wikström and Dolmen, 1990; Mayhew, 1990). The rational-interactionist model developed by van Dijk (1991, 1994) seeks to combine elements of offender-oriented strain theories and opportunity- or victim-oriented theories into a coherent theoretical framework, predicated upon the rational choice perspective (Cornish, Clarke, 1986).

In this integrated model the presence of motivated offenders is defined as the demand side of the «crime market». The availability of suitable and poorly protected targets is defined as the supply side of the same quasi-market[5].

People living below the subsistence level in, for instance, some African cities, will commit crimes for sheer biological survival. In other, less extreme situations the inclination to commit crimes is determined by the outcome of crude economic cost-benefit assessments. In our model the demand of crime within a population is determined by the number of people for whom the profits of illegal activities outweigh their costs. The profits are determined by the market price for stolen property. The opportunity costs of the involvement in crime are determined by the official minimum wages and wages in the black economy (Heineke, 1978). If legally or illegally paid wages are high, fewer people will rationally opt for the economic uncertainties of a life of crime[6]. The perceived risks to be caught and the expected type and severity of punishment — the punishment costs — must be added to the total costs of crime (Becker, 1968)[7].

From criminological studies it is known that young males are, for psychological and social reasons, more ready to take risks by committing offenses than others (Sutherland and Cressey, 1966; Hirschi and Gottfredson, 1983). Adolescents tend to overrate the long term benefits of crime and/or to underrate the punishment costs. If their financial situation is bleak, adolescents are a special risk group for becoming perpetrators of common crimes such as theft, burglary, robbery and assault.

The number of offenders and/or the frequency of their offending increases as long as the marginal illegal gains are larger than their marginal costs. If the (perceived) marginal net returns become smaller than the costs, the total number of offenses will start to drop. Conversely, the demand of crime is higher in populations with low minimum wages and/or high youth unemployment (ceteris paribus). In such countries even small gains are worth the risks of punishment.

The supply of criminal opportunities is primarily dependent of the sheer presence of suitable targets such as cars and other expensive consumer goods which can easily be removed. The supply of viable targets is further determined by the size and quality of social guardianship. The commission of crimes is hindered by various forms of social guardianship. Social control theory emphasises the exercise of social control by parents and other family members — the so-called handlers (Hirschi, 1969; Felson, 1994). Family cohesion seems a relevant supply factor for all types of crime predominantly committed by youngsters. Opportunity theory emphasises the importance of surveillance of property by housewives, neighbours or caretakers. The importance of social guardianship for the opportunities to offend differs per type of crime. Opportunities for burglary, for instance, might be greater for people living in easily accessible, detached houses in poorly integrated, anonymous neighbourhoods. Car theft and contact crimes may be stronger related to an outgoing lifestyle than to the quality of the neighbourhood.

If risks are high, potential victims respond by purposely improving their protection, for instance by implementing security measures, improving surveillance or even abstaining from outdoor activities in the evening. For the potential offenders such improved self-protection by potential victims increases the total costs per offense and therefore negatively affects the net gains of offending.

According to the rational-interactionist model, the potential offenders are permanently looking for opportunities to expand their numbers and frequencies of offending. The potential victims, however, reciprocate to the increasing losses from crime by taking extra security measures, thereby decreasing net gains. Potential victims tend to increase their level of self-protection up to the point whereat the marginal costs of security are larger than the losses prevented (the marginal benefits).

If the net gains of offenses are high, the total number of offenses tends to be high too. The behaviour of (potential) offenders is represented by a positive relationship between the level of crime and the net gains of offenses (the demand curve). If the number of offenses is high, the net gains tend to drop as a result of improved security. The behaviour of (potential) victims can be expressed by a inversed relationship between the level of crime and the offenders gains (the supply curve).

The level of crime tends to stabilise at the intersection of the demand and supply curves. The victims resign themselves to this level of crime since the additional costs of extra security or surveillance would be larger than the losses prevented. If the potential victims invest less in their security than would be rational, some trendsetters will start to increase their security and profit individually from this decision. Others will suffer from increased risks and eventually follow their example. In the event of potential victims overinvesting in their security, losses will soon drop to a level where such investments can no longer be justified financially. The levels of security will fluctuate around the point of equilibrium dictated by the intersection of the demand and supply curves.

At this volume, the offenders too enjoy a favourable relationship between the costs and benefits of their activities. If more offenders would enter the field or if the number of offenses carried out is increased, some of their activities would no longer be profitable, giving the costs and benefits involved. Their excessive offending would also provoke the potential victims into increasing their security. In time, this would lead to lower average yields and so to a reduction of the number of offenses to the previous level or lower. Given a certain level of economic deprivation and of criminal opportunities in a society, there is room for a quota of offenders/offenses[8].

As said, the number of offenses (the product of number of offenders and the frequency of their criminality) fluctuates around the level where the demand and supply curves meet. The equilibrium can be temporarily disturbed by external factors impinging upon the opportunity costs of crime — e.g. an economic recession — or upon the availability of viable targets — e.g. the introduction of new products such as the motor car or changes in social guardianship. Eventually a new equilibrium at a higher — or lower — level will be established. In our model interventions by the state — e.g. through a deterrent criminal policy t are viewed as external factors negatively affecting the net gains of offenses (Van Dijk 1994).

In this paper, we will test some hypotheses inferred from the rational-interactionist model by a cross-sectional analysis of the ICS victimisation rates and relevant background data collected in the same surveys or added from external sources. For a full-fledged empirical test of the model trend data must be available about the motivation to offend, the availability of targets and the investments in extra security or surveillance and about victimisation rates. Since at this stage such trend data are not available from the ICS, it is not yet possible to test hypotheses on the dynamic interplay between demand and supply factors on the one hand and crime rates on the other. We will instead look at the relations between some theoretically important demand and supply factors (including extra security) and crime/victimisation rates at a given point in time (1988 up to 1992).

FORMULATION OF HYPOTHESES

The present model can help to understand why both developing and ex-communist countries and some of the most affluent and welfare-minded countries in the West experience relatively high levels of crime. In the former countries, the high level of offenses may be caused by a poverty-induced higher demand of criminal gains. In the latter countries the ubiquity of viable targets of crime may be responsible for higher crime rates. It follows from the model that the two-dimensional correlations between affluence and crime rates will be weak or even non-existent globally.

The relations between affluence and crime rates are mediated by demand and supply factors which are themselves related to affluence in opposing directions. Affluence is inversely related to the inclination to offend. It is positively related to the presence of suitable targets. It is, again, inversely related to various forms of social control because in a context of lasting affluence various forms of social control and surveillance are weakened by a more individualistic and outgoing lifestyle. Finally, it follows from the model that more expensive protection measures are taken by populations suffering from high crime losses and related fears. Where crime is high, more people will see themselves as potential victims and take special measures to reduce their risks of criminal losses.

In order to understand the complex relationship between affluence and crime rates, a multivariate analysis must be made of the interplay between all essential factors listed above.

In figure 2 is depicted how the key factors at issue are related to each other according to the interactionist model.

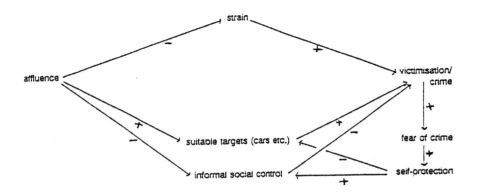

Most modern strain theorists do not assume a direct link between levels of prosperity and crime but rather between feelings of relative or cultural deprivation and crime (Young, 1986; see also Weatherburn, 1992). The present model supposes a direct link between the economic situation of a given population of young males and the motivation to offend. If (minimum) wages go up, the demand of crime goes down. However, the demand of crime may not decrease beyond a certain point in relatively affluent countries because the poorest young males may continue to experience strong feelings of relative deprivation (Runciman, 1972)[9]. In technical terms the demand of crime may be inelastic above a certain level of affluence. For this reason the macro relationship between affluence and crime is probably stronger among the less affluent, developing countries.

As said, the nature of the most relevant supply factors varies according to types of crime. Car related crimes, for instance, will probably be determined by car ownership rates and burglaries by type of housing and natural and/or professional surveillance. Contact crimes such as robberies will be largely determined by the strength of the demand factor since the opportunities to commit them — the presence of trespassers carrying cash or valuables — are probably a cross-national constant. Each crime type, then, is determined by a unique set of demand and supply factors and needs to be analysed separately.

Crime awareness and security measures too are largely crime-specific. Fear of burglary must be distinguished from fear of violent street crime[10]. Measures to prevent car theft are quite different from anti-burglary devices or precautions against street crimes.

In the ICS data-set some information is available about fear of burglary and fear of street crime. Information was also collected on the extent of conscious self-protection against household burglary. According to the rational-interactionist model, rates of fear of burglary and of anti-burglary devices will be higher in regions with high burglary rates[11].

Below are listed the hypotheses, deduced from the rational-interactionist model, about the cross-sectional relationships between affluence, demand factors, supply factors, protection factors and victimisation rates:

1.   Affluence indicators are inversely related to proxy measures of the inclination to commit crimes.

2.   Affluence indicators are positively related to ownership rates of cars and detached houses and to measures of an outgoing lifestyle.

3.   Affluence indicators are inversely related to proxy measures of family cohesion and natural surveillance.

4.   Proxy measures of the inclination to commit offenses are positively related to both overall and crime specific victimisation rates, controlling for other independent variables representing supply factors as indicated under 2 and 3.

111

5.   Measures of family cohesion and natural surveillance are inversely related to overall and crime-specific victimisation rates, controlling for other independent variables representing demand and supply factors.

6.   Rates of car ownership and measures of an outgoing lifestyle are positively related to overall and some crime specific victimisation rates (e.g. vehicle related crimes and contact crimes respectively), controlling for other independent variables representing demand and supply factors.

7.   Indicators of fear of burglary are related to burglary rates.

8.   Indicators of fear of burglary are related to the use of anti-burglary devices.

DATA-SET

The ICS data-set of the Criminological Institute of the University of Leyden currently comprises information about some 80,000 respondents. The information allows the computation of victimisation rates of thirty eight countries. Since in most countries sub-samples were drawn from the various regions in the country, it is possible to compute victimisation rates and other social measures of altogether 156 different regions across the world. Of these 114 are situated in industrialised countries, 13 in developing countries and 29 in Central or Eastern Europe.

Some straightforward hypotheses can be tested using data on 37 countries. For more complicated multivariate analyses a larger number of entities is to be preferred. It was therefore decided to analyse the data at the level of regions too. In most countries the samples were qualified according to so-called Nielsen's regions. Nielsen's regions are made up of provinces or states with common consumerist characteristics, typically made up of a few million of inhabitants. Such regions are well suited for testing criminological theories since most potential perpetrators and victims stay in the same region during their lifetime and most criminal interactions take place there as well. Since there is relatively little import or export of offenders or victims some of the complications of ecological studies of crime at the levels of neighbourhoods or towns do not apply[12].

The sample sizes of the regions vary between 100 and 1,000 (the typical region was represented by a sample of a few hundred respondents). In the statistical analyses a weight was introduced, assuring that regions represented by larger samples carried more weight in the calculations.

As said, in most developing countries the surveys were carried out among a sample from the population of a major city (usually the capital). A strong artificial bias is introduced in the global data-set, in the sense that regions with developing economies are over-represented among the most urbanised regions (linking urbanisation statistically to poverty).

112

This is by itself an important, statistical reason for analysing the global data-set, comprising all regions separately from the more homogeneous data set of the regions in the industrialised world. A second reason for separate analyses is that some items in the questionnaire used in the third world and in most of the Central and Eastern European countries were phrased marginally differently. In addition the latter surveys were carried out face to face in stead of by computer assisted telephone interviewing.

To sum up, results will be presented of multivariate analyses of the social correlates of crime rates (victimisation rates) of 156 regions across the world (114 regions of fully industrialised countries, 26 regions from central or eastern Europe and 19 regions with developing economies). Results will also be presented of the same analyses carried out on data from the 114 regions of industrialised countries only.

OPERATIONALISATION OF KEY CONCEPTS

Affluence was operationalised as the average score on a scale combining mean income in dollars and mean educational level (years at school). For each country the mean income and mean educational level was taken from external sources (UN Social Development Report, 1992)[13]. Regional indicators were subsequently calculated on the basis of the national averages and the regional rates of educational attainment and income according to the ICS data. The regional rates of mean income and mean educational level were strongly correlated. The resulting combined variable is called *affluence*.

According to modern strain theorists, the inclination to offend is stronger among people who are unemployed and/or feel economically disadvantaged. The ICS data set contains information on the employment situation of the respondents. A scale measuring social economic status was constructed using information on educational attainment, income, car ownership, home ownership and type of house (Van Dijk, 1991). In the second ICS, each respondent was also asked whether he or she was satisfied with the financial situation of his/her household.

An analysis was made of the relationships between various indicators of strain and crime rates. At variance with strain theory, the overall employment rate was inversely related to the crime rate. Crime rates are significantly higher in countries boasting low unemployment rates (-.45). In some of the poorest developing countries few people seem to define themselves as unemployed. The inversed relationship between unemployment and crime rates, however, was also found among the subset of industrialised countries.

The standard deviations of the SES scores per region were used as a measure of social inequality. This measure was related to the overall victimisation rate (+.31) in the global data-set but not among the industrialised countries (-.05).

113

Clear relations were found between the percentage of young males and crime (+.33) and between the percentages of people dissatisfied with their income and crime (+.13, n.s.). The strongest relations were found between the percentage of young males who are dissatisfied with their financial situation and the crime rate (+.43). The same results were found among the industrialised regions. Here the variables «young males» and «dissatisfaction with income» were not significantly related to crime but the variable «dissatisfied young males» was (+.20).

On the basis of these findings, the «demand of crime» was operationalised as the proportion of males below 30 who are dissatisfied with their financial situation. We have called this the *motivation* variable[14].

In the ICS data were collected on the ownership of cars, motorcars and bicycles by the household. *Ownership* rates will be used as opportunity measures for vehicle related crimes.

The first sweep of the ICS included one measure of social guardianship which was preserved (neighbours look out for suspicious signs without being asked to). This variable is called *natural surveillance*. In the second ICS some other questions were added. In the analyses are used a measure of *family cohesion* (frequency of family gatherings), and a three item-scale measuring *social control* (frequency of family gatherings, people in the neighbourhood usually help each other; neighbours keep an eye on things without being asked to do so). These three variables are highly inter-correlated.

In the ICS a question is asked on the frequency of going out. According to routine activity theory this feature measures the exposure to contact crimes as well as to burglary. In the second ICS the question was narrowed down to going out for recreational purposes (excluding professional activities). The new variable was more clearly related to contact crimes. It may represent, in addition to direct exposure to crime, the presence of leisure centres in the region. It may also be a proxy measure of alcohol consumption (a factor known to be related to crimes of violence). We have called this variable the *outgoing lifestyle* or *lifestyle/exposure* factor[15].

The ICS contains a question on type of housing. In the Western version of the ICS a distinction was made between detached, semidetached and terraced houses and flats/apartment buildings. In the face to face version the question was somewhat simplified, leaving only two answer categories (houses or flats/apartment buildings). The variable *house* represents the percentages living in either a detached or semi-detached house or a «house».

In both sweeps, respondents were asked how they rate their chances of being burgled over the next year. This item is called *fear of burglary*. In both sweeps respondents were also asked about their possession of a burglary alarm. In the second survey more questions were included about protection against burglary. The analysis was largely focused on *burglary alarms*.

STATISTICAL ANALYSES

The analysis of the constructed measures started with the calculation of correlation matrices. Subsequently multivariate analyses were carried out in order to test the causal models suggested by our theoretical perspective. For these path analyses we used the programme Lisrel VI (Jöreskog and Sörbom, 1983; see also Saris, 1984). The statistical relationships in the model are expressed in Bêta-coefficients (with values between -1 and +1). For each path model we will give the percentage of the variance in the dependent-variable (the victimisation rate) explained[16].

Although urbanisation as such is not a relevant factor according to the model, the external variable *urbanisation* was added as a control variable in all analyses. The level of urbanisation is known to be strongly related to crime levels. As we will see, the urbanisation-crime link is partly accounted for by some of the factors included in the model at issue.

In the path models Bêta-coefficients above .12 can be viewed as statistically significant (N=156). The coefficients found in the analyses of industrialised regions (n=114) must, of course, be somewhat higher to reach significance. As a general rule we will call coefficients between .12 and .25 weak, those between .25 and 40 clear or moderately strong and those above 40 strong.

RESULTS FOR THE OVERALL CRIME LEVEL

In this paragraph the results pertaining to the overall prevalence rates are presented.

In the data-set of all regions the variable *affluence* is weakly inversely correlated to the overall victimisation rate (r=-.23; p< 002). In the industrialised countries data-set the coefficient is +.22. Affluence is inversely related to overall victimisation rates in the global data-set and positively in the data-set of the industrialised countries.

This finding suggests that increased affluence brings down crime levels in a global perspective, in line with strain theories. In the most affluent countries, though, this dampening effect on the motivational side of crime is apparently more than offset by the crime-increasing growth of opportunity factors.

Hypotheses 1 to 6

In figure 3 the results are depicted of a path analysis as suggested by the hypotheses (all regions). The model explains 45 % of the variation in the victimisation rates. The inversed relationship between urbanisation and crime, caused by the over-sampling of large cities in developing countries, is not included in the model.

Figure 3:   *Results of a path analysis of the social correlates of overall victimisation rates: 156 regions representing 37 countries across the world ($x^2=1.31$; d.f.=2)*

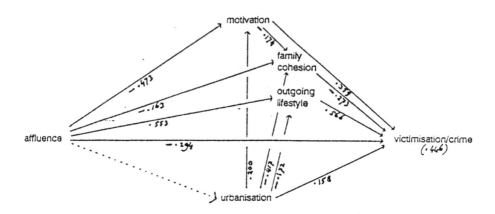

Hypotheses 1 and 4 are fully supported by the results. In affluent regions the rate of disgruntled young males is markedly lower (Bêta= -.473). As affluence goes up, fewer young people are inclined to commit crimes. The factor *motivation*, as defined by us, is clearly related to overall victimisation rates (Bêta= +.359).

Hypotheses 2 and 6 are also confirmed. Affluence is strongly related to an outgoing lifestyle and the latter factor is in turn strongly related to overall victimisation rates (Bêta=.566).

Hypotheses 3 and 5 are weakly supported by the findings. The correlation between *social control* and the victimisation rates is inversed as assumed, but not significantly so. Possibly a combined measure of family cohesion and two forms of natural surveillance catches two many different dimensions of social life, especially in a global perspective. In the final analysis, depicted in figure 3, the variable *social control* was replaced by the single issue variable *family cohesion*. In the resulting model FAMILY COHESION was clearly inversely related to the overall victimisation rate (Bêta=-.273). This result is fully in line with the hypotheses 3 and 5.

In a first analysis *affluence* was inversely related to *urbanisation*. As explained this is an artefact of the sampling design. In reality affluence is positively related to urbanisation (UNDP, 1992). As said, in the final model the causal relationship between affluence and urbanisation was not included. This did not in any significant way change the other relationships in the model. In the model *urbanisation* is positively related to *motivation* and inversely related to *family cohesion* and *lifestyle*. The impact of affluence on crime-inducing factors is partly mediated by the related process of urbanisation. City air seems to breed resentment among underprivileged young and to erode informal social control (family cohesion).

116

It is worth noting that *affluence* and *victimisation* are still inversely correlated in the empirical model controlling for relevant intermediary factors. Possibly this relationship would disappear if more sophisticated operationalizations of the motivation factor were used.

In figure 4 is depicted the result of the same path analysis applied to the data-set of industrialised countries. The most powerful model includes *natural surveillance* as an intermediary factor instead of *social control* or *family cohesion*. The model is again fairly strong. It explains 44 percent of the variance.

Figure 4:   *Results of a path analysis of the social correlates of overall victimisation rates: 114 regions in industrialised countries ($X^2=0.01$; d.f.=2)*

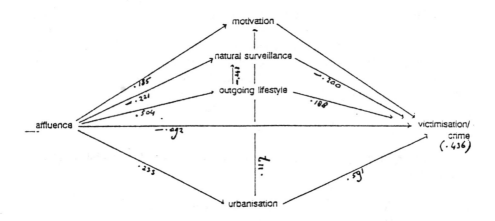

Most hypotheses are again confirmed but most coefficients are weaker. Interestingly, *affluence* is not inversely related to *motivation*. In fact, the percentage of dissatisfied young males tends to be larger in more affluent regions (Bêta=+.185). This finding lends support to the theory of relative deprivation[17]. *Motivation*, however, is not significanthy related to *victimisation*. In this empirical model feelings of relative deprivation do not act as a criminogenic factor.

In the final analysis we used *surveillance* rather than *social control* or *family cohesion*. In the alternative models too, inversed relationships were found between *affluence* and the intermediary variables and between the latter and crime. The relation between *surveillance* and *victimisation* is weakly inversed (-.200).

117

In the present model *affluence* is clearly related to *urbanisation*. *Urbanisation* is weakly related to *motivation* (.117).

In this model affluence is unrelated to victimisation (-.09), in contrast to the two-dimensional correlation (+.23). The latter finding shows that the positive relation between affluence and crime found in a two dimensional analysis disappears, if the impact of intermediary factors is adequately controlled for. Not affluence as such breeds crime but its repercussions on various dimensions of criminal opportunity.

RESULTS OF CRIME SPECIFIC ANALYSES

The social correlates of crime need to be analysed for each type of crime separately. We have carried out separate path analyses for the ten different types of crime included in the ICS questionnaire. Here will be presented the results on burglary, car theft and robbery. The left-side part of the models representing the interrelationships between the most relevant social characteristics of regions, is similar to that of the two main models, presented above. In all global models *motivation* is positively related to the crime specific victimisation rates. The relationships between other intermediary factors and crime are somewhat different for each type of crime. In general, the hypotheses are again confirmed.

Burglary

In figure 5 are depicted the main results of the analysis of the social correlates of burglary rates.

Figure 5:   *Results of a path analysis of the social correlates of burglary rates: 156 regions ($X^2=1.98$; d.f.=3)*

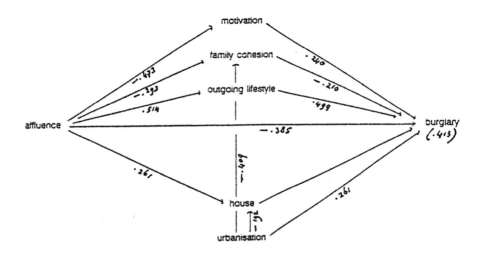

The results closely resemble those of the model analysing overall victimisation rates. In affluent regions there are less potential offenders but lower levels of social guardianship offer more opportunities of offending. The newly added factor *house* (representing ownership rates of detached or semi-detached houses) is related to *affluence,* as assumed in hypothesis 2, but unrelated to burglary rates. In the path analysis of the industrialised regions, the relationship between *house* and *burglary* was moderately strong (Bêta= +.340), though. Since living in a detached house implies less self-protection, hypothesis 5 is confirmed for industrialised regions. Regions wherein many families live in detached houses tend to have higher burglary rates.

The path model shows that affluence leads to increased opportunities for burglars.

Car theft

In figure 6 are depicted the main results on car theft.

Figure 6:   *Results of a path analysis of the social correlates of car theft rates: 156 regions (X^2=4.94; d.f.=5)*

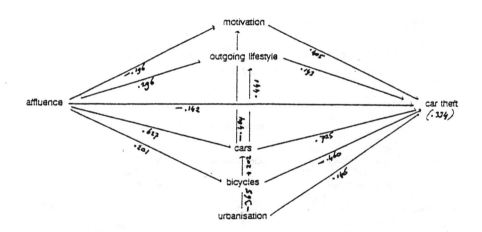

Ownership rates of cars and bicycles are related to *affluence.* The variable *car ownership* is strongly positively related to *car theft.* As was already known from previous analyses of the older ICS data, *bicycle ownership* is positively related to *car ownership* and inversely related to *car theft* (Van Dijk, Mayhew, Killias, 1990). The two-dimensional relationship between *car ownership* and *car theft* is statistically largely repressed by *bicycle own.Rates* (r=.13). The relationships are further complicated by the inversed relationships between urbanisation and both car and bicycle ownership rates

119

(-.155 and -.365 respectively). In the larger cities more people seem to rely on public transport. The model confirms hypothesis six: affluence clearly leads to higher car theft rates through the wider availability of ill-protected cars.

The inversed relationship between bicycle ownership rates and car theft can be interpreted in the following way (Mayhew, 1990; Van Dijk, Mayhew, 1993). In the ICS data cases of joy-riding are counted as car theft. In countries where young people are used to ride a bicycle from a very early age on, as is the case in The Netherlands, Germany and Sweden, adolescents are less strongly motivated to drive a car. In such countries the minimum age for acquiring a driving license tends to be higher too. For these reasons the motivation to commit joy-riding is probably weaker. In addition to this, there are plenty of easy opportunities to steal a bicycle in the North European countries. Those who are in need of transportation make do with a bicycle. The ample opportunities to commit bicycle theft act as another factor preventing joy-riding. These results nicely illustrate the complicated nature of the relationships between motivational factors, opportunity structures and crime specific victimisation rates.

The results are similar for the industrialised countries as a separate group but the relationship between motivation and car theft is weaker here (.161).

Robbery

The path model for robbery rates is depicted in figure 7.

Figure 7:   *Results of a path analysis of the social correlates of robbery rates: 156 regions ($X^2 = .401$; d.f.=6)*

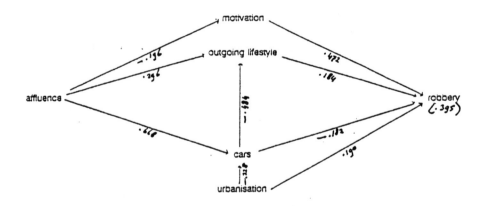

Motivation is strongly related to the dependent variable *robbery* (.472). The factor *lifestyle/exposure* is weakly related to *robbery*. None of the social control variables was related to *robbery* in the global data-set. Interestingly, *car ownership* was

120

found to be weakly inversely related to *robbery victimisation*. Possibly, the use of a car acts as a protective shield against robberies. More people making use of public transport or walking in the streets, might increase opportunities for robbery. This unexpected result is in line with hypothesis 5. Of all relevant factors, *motivation* is the only one clearly related to *robbery*.

The results for the industrialised regions showed that here urbanisation is the single most important factor.

Other crimes

The path analysis of victimisation rates for threats/assaults showed a model which in many respects mirrored that of overall victimisation rates. *Motivation* and *lifestyle* were both strongly related to *threats/assaults* (bêta's .58 and .40). *Family cohesion* was found to be weakly inversely related to *threats/assaults* (-.216). In this case affluence seems to decrease the motivation to offend but to lower thresholds for actually committing an offense. The main opportunity factor is likely to be the anonymous setting and heavy (beer) drinking in the entertainment areas of larger cities (see also Wikström and Dolmen, 1990; Field, 1990)[18].

Sexual incidents were related to the proportion of young people (< 30 years) and most of all to urbanisation.

The path analyses of the social correlates of the other types of property crime produced results similar to those for burglary and car theft. They are jointly related to the motivation factor and to relevant social control and target availability factors. Interestingly car damage and bicycle theft rates, however, are unrelated to the motivation variable. These two types of crime are exclusively related to relevant opportunity factors (car ownership and bicycle ownership).

To conclude, the levels of robbery are determined largely by the deprivation-induced motivation to offend. Assaults and most types of property crimes are determined by a combination of motivational and opportunity factors. Bicycle thefts and car vandalism are largely determined by specific opportunity structures and related sub-cultures of offending.

FEED BACK LOOPS

According to the model potential victims react to their victimisation risks with rationally determined levels of self-protection which help to control crime. Put differently, the model assumes a negative feed back loop stabilizing crime rates at a given level, ceteris paribus[19]. According to the model populations suffering from relatively high victimisation rates, will invest most in their protection[20].

Hypotheses on the feed back loops must ideally be tested with time series analyses. As said, the present ICS data-set does not yet allow this. The data do allow, however, a preliminary analysis of the cross-sectional relationships between victimisation rates, risk awareness (fear of crime) and the implementation of security measures. For a more extensive analysis of the relationship between crime, fear of crime and self-protection we refer to other publications (Cusson, 1990; Skogan, 1987; Warr, Balvig, Weinberg, 1987; Weinstein, 1989; Van Dijk, 1994[11]).

We have first analysed the repercussions of burglary. Included in the analysis is the rate of victimisation by successful *burglaries* (excluded are attempted burglaries). *Fear of burglary* is represented by an item measuring the perceived likelihood of a burglary in one's house. Security is represented by the rate of people owning a burglar *alarm*. Since the burglar alarm ownership rates are very low in all developing countries we will present here the results of the analysis on the subset of industrialised regions.

Figure 8:   *The relationships among industrialised nations between affluence, level of urbanisation, proportion of detached houses, burglary victimisation, fear of burglary and ownership of burglar alarms; results of a path analysis (N=114); X^2=5.50; d.f.=10*

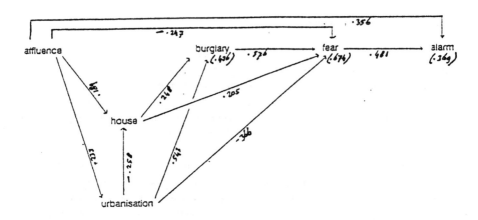

The comprehensive path model explains 44 % of the variance in burglary rates, 67 % of the variance in the fear of burglary rates and 37 % of the variance in burglar alarm rates. The relationships on the left of the path-model are similar to the ones in the path model explaining burglary rates (see discussion on figure 5). Added are the strong relations between *burglary* rates and *fear of burglary* and between the latter variable and *burglary alarms*. Hypotheses 7 and 8 are clearly confirmed. There can be no doubt that collective levels of expensive self-protection are propelled by a heightened risk awareness in response to high burglary rates, as predicted by the rational-interactionist model.

The other relationships on the right of the present path model are also worth commenting upon. In accordance with the model affluence is independently related to the ownership of alarms. In the global analysis this positive relationship is even stronger (.555). In poorer countries households can ill afford the purchase of an expensive alarm. In these countries, however, other measures such as high fences, grilled windows and sound locks are very common. The feed back loop triggered by high losses from burglaries is not absent but takes a different, less expensive form. The nature of the victims' rational response to crime losses seems to be determined by prevailing economic conditions.

fear of burglary is related to *burglary* and also to known risk factors like *detached house* and *urbanisation*. These results are in line with the notion that fear of crime is a rational response to objective crime-specific threats. Interestingly, affluence is weakly inversely related to *fear of burglary*. This finding gives some support to the competing notion that fear of crime has other social sources besides crime — such as anxiety about political or economic prospects. By and large the results are concurrent with the idea of risk awareness/fear of crime as a rational response to crime.

The rational interactionist model also applies to crimes of violence. In affluent regions people go out for recreation in the evening much more often. As demonstrated above, this feature of an affluent lifestyle entails higher levels of violent crime. This effect can be counteracted by a heightened level of precautionary measures.

In the ICS data were collected on the taking of precautionary measures during outdoor visits in the evening (the last time you went out, did you avoid certain places or people out of fear of crime?). According to the model more people will employ such precautionary practices in regions with high levels of threats/assaults and/or sexual incidents. The analysis bore out that precautionary behaviour is strongly related to the rate of violent crime (e.g. robbery rates by avoidance: r=+.68; n=156). High rates of violent crime engender an increased risk awareness and readiness to take precautionary measures. Whether such avoidance behaviour reduces contact crimes at the macro level remains to be seen. As we have demonstrated, there is some empirical support, however, for the idea that the collective use of cars as means of transportation diminishes the number of robberies. If large parts of the population demonstrate avoidance behaviour this factor may likewise affect robbery rates. Evidence for such negative feed back loops was found by Liska and Warner (1991).

The countermeasures against high rates of burglary or street crimes do not bring about rates which lie below the global average. If such measures are taken by a sufficiently large proportion they will negatively affect the costs/benefits assessments of would be offenders. The opportunities of crime will be somewhat reduced. The level of crime will also be somewhat reduced and/or at least be stabilised at a given level. If burglary rates would fall substantially, potential victims are likely to become more relaxed about their self-protection. In due time the burglary rates will be on the rise again. According to our model a fall far below the global average is not to be expected.

The data on burglary do allow an indirect test of the impact of improved security on the costs of committing burglaries. In the survey respondents are not just asked whether their houses were burgled but also whether someone tried to do so in vain (burglary without entry). If burglar alarms act as a barrier to burglaries the proportion of all burglaries which failed should be higher in regions with high rates of burglar alarms. The results of an analysis confirmed this additional hypothesis. If the variable *proportion uncompleted burglaries* is included in the path analysis, the variable *alarms* and the new variable *proportion failed burglaries* are weakly related (+.212). In other words, if more people install alarms, a larger proportion of all burglaries fail. Similar results are found in an analysis of the relationships between a scale of anti-burglary measures and the ratio between uncompleted and completed burglaries. Regions with higher average scores on the anti-burglary measures scale tend to have higher proportions of failed burglaries. These results suggest the existence of an effective negative feed back loop, contributing to a better control of crime in the long term.

DISCUSSION

The results of the path analyses are for the most part in accordance with the hypotheses derived from the rational interactionist model. The model offers an explanation for the ambiguous relationships between affluence and levels of crime. In a global perspective, increasing levels of affluence seem to reduce the motivation to commit offenses. In the terminology of the model, the demand of crime is weaker. This effect is the most powerful with regard to robberies, threats/assaults and car thefts. At the same time affluence and the accompanying urbanisation process increase the opportunities for car-related crimes, threats/assaults and burglaries along various ways. The upshot is that these types of crimes are not, or not substantially, reduced by rising levels of affluence, although demand of crime is diminished by better social conditions. In the case of robbery, affluence does not seem to create new opportunities. Affluence, on the contrary, increases self-protection against robbery by changing the routine activity patterns of transportation (more use of cars). As a consequence, affluence and robbery rates are inversely related. In an international macro perspective robbery can be characterised as a poor man's crime. Or, to put it technically, as a demand-driven type of crime. In poorer countries a relatively large part of all crimes committed against individuals or households is made up of such demand-driven crimes.

The results explain why most other types of crime are unrelated to affluence. If affluence goes up the rates of burglaries and various types of theft are reduced by a contraction of the pools of motivated offenders. However, the rates are simultaneously driven up by the greater opportunities for profitable offending[21]. Car vandalism is an example of a type of crime which is exclusively driven by opportunities. It is an 'expressive' type of crime which people living in poorer conditions can ill afford. This type of crime is therefore positively related to affluence.

In the industrialised world, then, crimes like burglary, minor thefts and assaults and car vandalism are driven up by increased opportunities. Victimisation by such crimes can be viewed as the down-side of affluence. In the terminology of our model, such crimes are defined as opportunity or supply-driven. In the industrialised world a relatively large part of all crimes committed against individuals or households are supply-driven vehicle-related crimes and burglaries. Street robberies committed by young people without any prospects of a legal income are relatively rare. Both the composition of the crime package and the causal factors of crime differ sharply from those in poorer countries.

The social background and nature of the crime problem in industrialised countries is different, even if its size is roughly the same as in countries with developing economics.

The model should now be transformed into a formal theory and put to more rigorous empirical tests. A replication of the analyses on other sophisticated data-sets — e.g. regional or time series data collected in the course of national victimisation surveys — is called for. The model should also be tested with data on crime against businesses and on investments in security by the business sector. Largely unexplored is the question whether and how crime specific opportunity structures shape the size and distribution of *other* types of crime. The quality of the protection of household property may, for instance, effect crimes against businesses and vice versa.

Beyond a certain level, types of opportunity-driven crimes increase risk awareness and lead to more expensive forms of self-protection. According to the model this spontaneous negative feed back mechanism brings about a stabilisation of the relevant types of crime. The realistic risk awareness of households and firms in high risk areas and their related willingness to invest in technical or behavioral self-protection constitute adaptive social mechanisms (Bartel, 1975; Clotfelter, 1977; Cusson, 1990; Van Dijk, 1994). In victimological criminology such manifestations of sensible caution have been insufficiently distinguished from emotional fears as part of mental trauma (Van Dijk, 1994[II]). In future victimological research the underlying pragmatism rather than the emotional and punitive aspects of the public's response to crime should be given due attention (Skogan, 1987; Bennett, 1990; Cusson, 1990; Van Dijk, 1994[II]). More research ought also to be done on the effectiveness and efficiency of situational crime prevention at the level of individuals, communities and larger populations (Cusson, 1993; Clarke, 1994).

According to our present understanding (potential) offenders in developing countries are willing to commit crimes even if the net yields are very small. In this situation of a demand-driven crime problem, there is limited scope for effective crime prevention by potential victims through improved self protection. The hard core of offenders will always create their own opportunities of crime, regardless of investments in security. In more affluent countries, the inclination to offend is more opportunistic. Potential victims can influence the decision-making of potential offenders by limiting the net yields through improved self-protection. In the light of our results, the rational-interactionist notion of a negative feed back through increased self-protection seems to be more applicable to the crime situation in industrialised countries than to that in the third world (see also Bennett, 1991).

In the first paragraph, league tables were presented of national victimisation percentages. The crime rates of individual countries can now be interpreted in the framework of the rational interactionist model.

According to the empirically tested model, presented in figure 4, overall crime rates are predominantly determined by:

a. the percentage of dissatisfied young males (*motivation*);
b. the extent of outdoor leisure activities (*lifestyle/exposure*);
c. the degree of affluence, independently of the factors listed above (*affluence*);
d. urbanisation.

Secondary determining factors are the cohesion of family life and the extent of natural surveillance among neighbours.

A multiple regression analysis was made of the national victimisation rates as dependent variables and *lifestyle/exposure*, *motivation* and *affluence* as independent variables[22]. These three independents explain 53 % of the variance in the national crime rates. We have subsequently calculated the predicted victimisation rate of each country on the basis of the regression coefficients. In figure 9 is depicted to which extent individual national crime rates conform to or diverge from the rates predicted by the model.

Figure 9: *Graphic representation of differences between actual national victimisation rates and those predicted by a regression model using lifestyle/exposure, criminal motivation and affluence as independent variables (deviations to the left indicating lower rates than predicted and those to the right higher rates)*

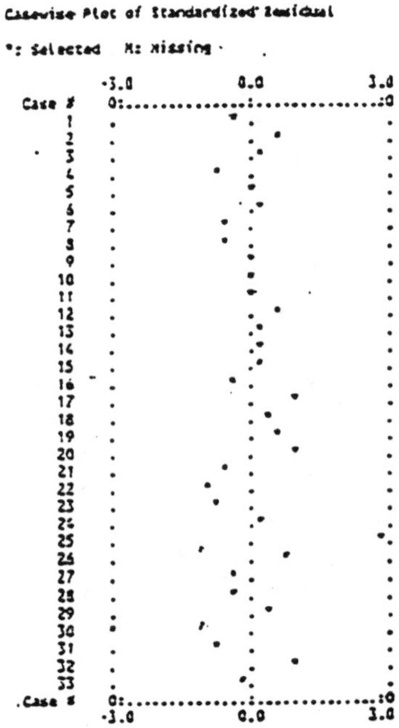

Case #	@VICTIM	*PRED	*RESID	
1	.23	.2551	-.0226	England and Wales
2	.27	.2326	.0416	Netherlands
3	.24	.2217	.0171	Germany
4	.15	.2042	-.0508	Switzerland
5	.18	.1839	-.00	Belgium
6	.17	.1643	+.00	France
7	.16	.1952	-.0381	Norway
8	.17	.2127	-.0402	Finland
9	.23	.2199	.01	Spain
10	.21	.2118	+.00	Sweden
11	.25	.2623	-.00	Italy
12	.27	.2298	.0393	USA
13	.27	.2552	.0155	Canada
14	.27	.2511	.0184	Australia
15	.30	.2946	.00	New Zealand
16	.09	.1122	-.0222	Japan
17	.29	.2195	.0676	Poland
18	.26	.2336	.0219	Tjechoslowakia
19	.16	.1220	.0371	Georgia
20	.29	.2313	.0611	Moscow
21	.23	.2713	-.0423	Slovenia
22	.26	.3175	-.0614	Estonia
23	.22	.2816	-.0576	Indonesia
24	.23	.2232	.00	Costa Rica
25	.58	.3882	.1934	Uganda
26	.31	.2599	.0508	Brazil
27	.22	.2526	-.0291	Philippines
28	.28	.3022	-.0212	Egypt
29	.39	.3669	.0201	Argentina
30	.09	.3058	-.2193	India
31	.33	.3882	-.0552	South Africa
32	.34	.2748	.0616	Tanzania
33	.37	.3756	-.0100	Tunesia
Case #	@VICTIM	*PRED	*RESID	

Figure 9 shows that the national crime rates of most countries are fairly accurately predicted by the model (with a margin of five points in either direction). The actual rates of most nations can largely be explained in terms of a simple model including three factors (percentages of dissatisfied young males, frequencies of outdoor visits in the evening and level of affluence). To the extent that some nations experience relatively low actual crime rates, as is for example the case with Belgium and Sweden, the explanation for this can be found in relatively low national scores on one or more of the three factors included in the model. The same applies for countries with relatively high actual rates such as Tanzania, Costa Rica, Canada, Australia, New Zealand and Spain. Considering their criminogenic features as defined by the model, the high crime rates of the latter countries are to be expected. There is no need to look for special causes of crime in unique social characteristics or policies of these countries.

The national rate of India is much lower than predicted by the model. Other nations with rates more than five points lower than predicted are Switzerland, Estonia, Indonesia and South Africa. In these countries factors external to the model somehow exert a positive impact up on the level of crime. It is noteworthy that this group includes both high crime countries (Estonia and South Africa) and low crime countries (Switzerland and Indonesia).

In Kampala (Uganda) the national crime rate is much higher than predicted. Other nations with substantially higher rates than those predicted by the model are Poland, Moscow (Russia), Rio (Brazil), and Dar es Salam (Tanzania). Part of the explanation for the deviations of the latter three can probably be found in the fact that the samples were drawn from a large city.

As mentioned, each national victimisation rate can be understood in relation to the national scores on the key factors. To allow a better understanding of national victimisation rates, we have depicted in figure 10 the rates of the three criminogenic factors in z-scores, together with the actual and predicted victimisation rates.

127

Figure 10:   *National rates of criminogenic social characteristics according to the regression model in z-scores and actual and predicted overall victimisation rates*

	Motivation	Going out	Affluence	Victim. rate	Predicted rate
England/Wales	-.74	1.27	.78	.23	.26
Netherlands	-.99	.96	.66	.27	.23
Germany	-.78	.76	.86	.24	.22
Switzerland	-.79	.78	1.27	.15	.20
Belgium	-.93	-.05	.56	.18	.18
France	-.67	-.39	.83	.17	.16
Norway	-.79	.87	1.52	.16	.20
Finland	-.84	.72	.96	.17	.21
Spain	-.52	-.41	-.30	.23	.22
Sweden	-.72	.78	1.16	.21	.21
Italy	-.76	.39	-.05	.25	.24
USA	-.52	1.57	1.95	.27	.23
Canada	-.43	1.56	1.44	.27	.26
Australia	-.72	1.26	.87	.27	.25
New Zealand	-.40	1.35	.32	.30	.29
Japan	-.96	-1.02	.94	.09	.11
Poland	1.13	-1.81	-.41	.29	.22
Czechoslovakia	.40	-.64	-.00	.26	.23
Georgia	-.11	-2.47	-.24	.16	.12
Moscow	1.01	-1.39	-.29	.29	.23
Slovenia	-.38	.118	-.59	.23	.27
Estonia	1.13	-.07	-.47	.26	.32
Indonesia	.05	-.35	-1.07	.22	.28
Costa Rica	-.78	-.55	-.81	.23	.22
Uganda	1.10	.29	-1.65	.58	.39
Brazil	.15	-.65	-.85	.31	.26
Philippines	.51	-.98	-.75	.22	.25
Egypt	.60	-.46	-1.13	.28	.30
Argentina	1.46	.75	-.25	.39	.37
India	.57	-.75	-1.60	.09	.31
South Africa	3.53	-1.01	-.90	.33	.39
Tanzania	-.16	-.73	-1.59	.34	.27
Tunisia	1.36	.23	-1.18	.37	.38

Source : ICS 1989/1992

As can be seen in table 10 nearly all developing and ex-communist countries have relatively many dissatisfied young males in their midst. South Africa is an extreme case. The proportion of potential offenders is lowest in the Netherlands and Japan, countries with the least socio-economic inequality according to *UN* indicators (UNDP, 1992).

People tend to go out more often in developed countries, notably in New World countries. Outdoor leisure activities are the least common in Spain, France and the ex-communist countries. Georgia, where a civil war was raging at the time of the study, is an extreme case, with very few people leaving their houses in the evening.

The rates for affluence — a measure for GNP per capita and
educational attainment — holds few surprises. New World and West European c
show the highest rates (with Spain and Italy at the lower end within Western)
By and large the crime rates of most countries can be accounted for by their
in terms of the three key criminogenic factors.

NATIONAL CRIME PROFILES

In order to diagnose national crime problems, each nation
characterised in terms of the sizes of its crime specific victimisation rate:
criminogenic features according to our model. Such diagnosis would show
both the phenomenology of the crime problem and its social context. An
attempt to make such a comprehensive criminological diagnosis, was mad
our Japanese ICS partners, Fumiko Takasugi (1991).

We have started our analysis with carrying out a factor analysis o
crime specific victimisation prevalence rates and the national rates for
motivation, lifestyle/exposure, car ownership, bicycle ownership, motorcy
and urbanisation (n=37)[23]. After a varimax rotation five factors were four
sense in terms of the model. Together they explain 82.6 % of the)
variables[24]. This factor analysis shows which crime specific victimis
criminogenic factors go together at the level of nations.

The first factor is defined by high loadings of the variables ca
vandalism and lifestyle/exposure. This factor seems to represent *opporti
crime*. The second factor shows high loadings of the variables burgla:
and, to a lesser extent, of the variable theft from cars. The variable u
loading of .31.

This second factor is rather difficult to interpret since nor
criminogenic factors loads on it[25]. As is known from the crime
burglary is related to unique opportunity structures, which are n
analysis. We have called this factor the *property crime factor*.

The third factor is again quite clear cut and easy to i
loadings are those of the variables motivation, robbery and threats/
of car theft is .46. This factor clearly represents the dimension of
violent crimes.

The fourth factor represents bicycle ownership/*bicycle*
a negative loading of .60. The fifth factor represents motorcycle
of motorcycles.

As a final step in our analysis, we have calculated for
on the five factors presented above (in z-scores). This overview
criminological profile of each individual country in a global per
given in figure 11.

Figure 11: National scores on five criminological dimensions found in a factor analysis of crime-specific victimisation rates and some criminogenic features

	Opp. driv. petty crime	Property crime	Depr. driven violent crime	Bicycle theft	Motocycle theft
England/Wales	1.14	-.17	-.42	-1.22	-.68
Netherlands	1.02	.30	-.19	2.20	-.16
Germany	1.07	-.05	-.46	.35	-.88
Switzerland	.01	-.92	-.76	.68	.86
Belgium	.43	-.67	-.59	-.09	-.05
France	.61	-.65	-.50	-1.13	.13
Norway	.47	-.92	-.26	.24	-.53
Finland	.37	-.75	-.31	1.10	-.71
Spain	.45	-.32	.00	-1.29	.15
Sweden	.62	-.64	.00	1.59	.11
Italia	.87	-.55	-.50	-.82	2.11
USA	1.69	.34	.28	-.37	-.60
Canada	1.38	.25	.00	.08	-.80
Australia	1.39	.36	-.18	-.82	-.65
New Zealand	1.52	.44	.20	-.08	-.23
Japan	-.85	-1.40	-1.00	.48	.82
Poland	-.50	-.27	.44	.71	.28
Czechoslovakia	-.12	-.09	.01	1.16	-.16
Georgia	-1.21	-.75	-.56	-2.11	-.52
Moscow	-1.04	.33	.53	.11	-1.16
Slovenia	.18	-.07	-.87	.27	.14
Estonia	-.55	-.12	1.01	1.74	-.04
Indonesia	-1.06	.12	-.85	.56	1.82
Costa Rica	-.99	.68	-1.20	.70	-.42
Uganda	-.74	3.63	.70	.74	-.17
Brazil	-.79	-.77	1.87	.15	-.25
Philippines	-1.92	-.00	-.46	.06	-1.00
Egypt	-1.13	.39	-.36	-.80	-.37
Argentina	.50	-.32	2.36	-.88	2.62
India	-1.89	-.75	-.84	-1.12	-.84
South Africa	-.45	-.50	3.47	.76	-1.42
Tanzania	.37	2.84	-.99	-1.42	.15
Tunisia	-.84	1.07	.46	-.10	2.49

In a global perspective the crime situation in England/Wales, for example, is
acterised by a moderately high score for opportunity-driven petty crime/vandalism
a low score for bicycle theft. By contrast the crime problem in a country like
nd is characterised by a fairly high score on deprivation-driven violent crime and
h score for bicycle theft.

We will not try to comment on the crime profiles of each individual nation.
general findings seem noteworthy. Countries with high scores on the first factor
New World countries, England, the Netherlands and Germany. In these relatively
nt countries, young people commit opportunistic crimes. Besides car vandalism,
forms of petty crime are probably endemic here as well. In the case of the
lands, bicycle theft, for instance, has become a national plague. Unlike most West
ean countries, the New World countries show relatively high scores on the
ty crime factor as well (a factor characterised by high burglary rates).

Some developing and ex-communist countries, notably South Africa, Argentina, Brazil, Uganda, Russia, Estonia and Poland, show the highest scores on the third factor, representing deprivation-induced crimes of violence. The nature of crime in these countries is probably more demand-driven across the board. The crime problem of some other countries with developing economies is characterised by high scores on property crimes rather than on the third factor (Tanzania, Tunisia and Costa Rica). Uganda scores high on both factors.

The national crime profiles must — of course — be interpreted with caution by national experts and preferably be brought in relation to other sources of information. The scores in figure 10 of some nations must be checked against other sources because they may be affected by missing data or by our sampling design.

RESPONSES AND POLICIES

According to police figures, recorded crime has risen almost universally in the eighties (United Nations, 1993). In our view this upward trend is partly caused by socio-economic adversity of large sections of the population in notably Africa, South America and Eastern Europe and partly by the greater availability of suitable targets and a breakdown of traditional forms of informal social control in urban environments across the world.

Households and individuals afflicted by high crime rates are well aware of their objective risks and respond rationally by taking various kinds of self-protection measures. The collective taking of such measures alters the opportunity structures for specific types of crime. In some affluent countries, burglary rates are found to be stabilised or reduced by high levels of security at neighbourhood level (Forrester et al, 1990; Lindsay and McGilles, 1986). In the long term national crime rates of affluent nations will be stabilised by these spontaneous counter measures.

Statistics of crimes recorded by the police show a incessant increase of most types of crime since the sixties in most Western countries. National victimisation surveys, however, often show a less bleak picture. National victimisation percentages have increased just slightly over the past ten years in both the Netherlands and the USA.

In the USA victimisation levels for most types of crime have in fact been relatively high for many years. Risk awareness and security levels have also been relatively high. According to the national crime surveys, non-violent crimes have been stable for over a decade (Skogan, 1991). This remarkable phenomenon may be a current example of a national crime level stabilised by improved self-protection by middle class households and businesses as a response to high exposure to criminal victimisation[26].

Somewhat speculatively, rising crime rates in several West European countries Canada, Australia and New Zealand in the early nineties have been caused by an increased demand of crime, due to economic adversity (see also Field, 1990). Since target availability did not substantially drop and the extent of self-protection is still modest compared to that in the USA, increased demand has resulted in higher crime rates. In these countries levels of self-protection are therefore likely to increase in the years to come. The upward trend in community-based crime prevention and in professional forms of surveillance and state-of-the-art electronic security devices in cars, houses, shops and other firms will probably lead to a stabilisation of property crime in the late nineties (ceteris paribus, that is if youth unemployment rates do not go up further).

In Central and Eastern Europe the restructuring of the economy is accompanied by high rates of youth unemployment. To the extent that young males cannot find jobs or earn low wages, the demand of crime will remain high. The factor seems currently to be the strongest in Estonia, Poland and Russia (see figure 10). At the same time, many more luxury goods such as cars become available to the newly rich (especially in Hungary and the Czech Republic). The present crime boom in this part of Europe is unlikely to come to a halt in the short run, since full employment and minimum wages for adolescents are not within reach. Neither are private citizens and business owners much inclined to invest parts of their newly acquired fortunes in self-protection measures. The usual negative feed back mechanism of crime may be somewhat delayed in a situation of rapid economic transition.

POLICY IMPLICATIONS

The results of the regression analysis based on the interactionist model can be used to make estimates of national and local crime rates. On the basis of information on the rate of subjectively deprived young males, frequency of outdoor visits and GNP per capita, fairly accurate estimates can be made of the crime situation anywhere in the world without carrying out a victimisation survey. As mentioned before, the results of our analyses must be interpreted with caution. The data of some countries are dated and some data were missing altogether and had to be estimated on the basis of averages of similar countries. It must also be born in mind that the victimisations of private persons make up only part of the total crime problem. Crimes against businesses[27] and state institutions and so-called victimless crimes are outside the scope of this analysis. With these reservations made, the tested model may yet provide some guidance for policy making.

A CRITIQUE OF CONVENTIONAL CRIME POLICIES

If crime is seen as a pressing problem, governments traditionally intervene by increasing the certainty and/or severity of punishment. In terms of the present model such interventions are directed at the demand side of the problem. In many countries a distinct political trend towards more punitive policies is now in evidence.

In the ICS data-set, the support of severe punishment of offenders is strongly related to levels of affluence. Punitiveness is the highest in the less-affluent, crime-ridden regions of the third world. In the industrialised West the public tends to favour a more innovative crime policy promoting non-custodial sanctions (Van Dijk, 1994[11]). The USA features as the most notable exception to this rule. Although affluence and levels of educational attainment are high, the American public exhibits a preference for long prison sentences. In this, public opinion in the USA differs strikingly from that in Western Europe. The public in central and eastern Europe is also more in favour of imprisonment than the inhabitants of the European Union.

In countries like Brazil, Argentina and South Africa, where crime is mainly driven by a strong demand for illegal gains, governments may have few other options to reduce crime in the short term than to try to deter known and potential offenders through harsh punishment. If many young males suffer from severe economic hardship, improved self-protection is unlikely to have much impact, e.g. on the activities of young street robbers or burglars.

In line with the «economics of crime» approach of Becker (1968) rational-interactionism assumes that decision making by potential and recidivist offenders is influenced by punishment costs. However, it remains doubtful whether tougher criminal policies can substantially and permanently reduce crime. The research evidence indicates that above certain minimum levels extra police or more severe sentences exert limited additional deterrent or incapacitation effects on (potential) offenders (see e.g. Von Hirsch, 1988; Von Hofer and Thamm, 1989; Thomas and Edelman, 1988; Van Tulder, 1994). As is known from many evaluation studies the infliction of severe punishment upon young offenders tends to have counterproductive effects on recidivism rates. The public's demand of severe punishment in response to crime waves may exacerbate existing crime problems and thus constitute a positive instead of a negative feed back loop.

Rehabilitative measures such as intensive probation supervision or community service orders have better prospects in terms of recidivism reduction, but their prospects for actually reducing crime seem rather limited too. The present model assumes that in an area with a given labour market and opportunity structure there is room for a certain quota of active offenders. If the number of offenders exceeds this quota the equilibrium is disturbed and potential victims will step up their self-protection. If the quota is not reached as a result of successful rehabilitation programmes of young offenders, newcomers from the same socio-economic strata will rapidly take the place of their reformed brethren (the so-called *replacement phenomenon*). The rational-interactionist model does not leave much scope for optimism about the preventive potential of extra investments in criminal justice systems above reasonable levels. In the long term the solution for demand driven crime problems in countries like Brazil, South Africa and Argentina will probably have to come primarily from economic growth and a better socio-economic integration of young males in particular.

INTERVENING AT THE SUPPLY SIDE

According to the interactionist model the level of crime in affluent countries is jointly determined by motivational factors and criminal opportunities. As a consequence, governments in such countries can choose between intervention directed at the demand side or at the supply side of the crime problem. Extra punitive measures per se are unlikely to reduce crime for the reasons mentioned above. In a situation of nearly unlimited opportunities for crime, a somewhat higher risk of punishment is unlikely to affect substantially and permanently the cost-benefit assessments of dissatisfied, risk taking young males. Temporary reductions of certain types of crime due to highly visible law and order initiatives may create a security illusion among potential victims and persuade them to reduce their investments in self-protection. Such side-effects may make successful law enforcement policies counterproductive in the long term (Cook, 1986; Van Dijk, 1994). The possibilities of successful forms of primary prevention among high risk groups are limited too. In affluent societies feelings of relative deprivation are difficult to dispel with employment or welfare policies. Socialisation and informal social control patterns will also be difficult to change. The trend towards a more individualistic lifestyle will most probably continue in most Western countries.

In affluent societies interventions on the supply side hold the promise of a better return on investment than those on the demand side of the crime market. Without fundamental changes in the opportunity structures of crime, crime rates in Western industrialised countries seem to be policy resistant. Rather than just expanding punitive policies, governments should seriously consider to promote and regulate the use of elementary security measures (Clarke, 1980). Instead of exclusively expanding the criminal justice system, governments should encourage the spontaneous social trend towards improved self-protection by means of legislation and fiscal or subsidy policies. Governments should help potential victims to help themselves in the interest of society (Field and Hope, 1989). Topical examples are the obligatory application of immobilisation techniques in motorcars, sophisticated alarm devices in houses, company offices and public buildings and closed circuit television in private and semipublic spaces. In addition, governments should promote community-based initiatives and the employment of masses of caretakers, wardens, conductors, car park attendants etcetera as a means to control petty crime (Willemse, 1994). By recruiting for such jobs among the long term unemployed such policies can help to reduce unemployment as well. Also, police forces should routinely visit crime victims and advise them on how to prevent repeat victimisation (Winkel, 1991; Pease and Farrell, 1993; Polvi et al, 1990).

Insurance companies are ideally placed to collect, analyse and transfer information about the costs of crime and crime prevention. In many areas of crime, governments should invite leading insurance companies to better exploit their data-banks and determine reasonable minimum standards of security for private and commercial clients. Such standards can help to prevent temporary cut backs on security in times of declining crime rates. They can also help to prevent the phenomenon of security free riders (companies profiting from the investments in collective security of their neighbours). Governments should set up and maintain strategic alliances with the insurance industry for this purpose.

In some instances victimisation risks may be shifted towards the least protected property, owned by the poorer parts of the population. This so-called *displacement phenomenon* is often raised as an argument against situational crime prevention. In most situations displacement towards other targets or criminal techniques is only partial (Hesseling, 1994). Nevertheless, a redistribution of crime risks is indeed socially undesirable if it hurts the most vulnerable sections of the public. But this possible side effect should not be taken as a justification for a laisser faire policy on situational crime prevention. On the contrary, it presents a cogent argument for government interventions. If the burden of crime tends to shift towards the most vulnerable section of the public, such unwanted side effects of the rational choices of potential victims should be actively counteracted upon by governments. Crime prevention advice and support for those incapable to satisfy their own elementary security needs is a primary obligation of the modern welfare state and its related institutions (such as state schools and social housing estates). For instance, social housing estates must be financially assisted in making their estates safer. Security requirements in the workplace should be included in statutory safety regulations and be an issue in negotiations about labour conditions in banks, petrol stations, hospitals, department stores, leisure centres etcetera.

As said, the proposed preventive policies are likely to offer in the long term a better return on investment than further one-sided expansions of police forces and prison departments alone. To this end preventive policies must go beyond the current demonstration projects of local governments and the scattered initiatives of voluntary groups or insurance companies. A veritable crime prevention policy of both national and local government in collaboration with the business sector is called for.

The same arguments apply, with some qualifications, to the situation in central and eastern European countries. Governments in some of these countries are pressurised by the electorate into a punitive approach towards the growing crime problem. The present model suggests that such a policy must at least be supplemented by the promotion of preventive measures. In a European perspective the present criminal policies in the East are already relatively punitive (as evidenced by the higher rates of prisoners per capita). This policy requires high expenditures with dubious returns in terms of crime reduction. At the same time the countries in the east are lagging far behind in crime prevention efforts. In the collaboration between West and East European countries in the area of crime control more attention must be given to both offender oriented and situational preventive approaches.

Situational crime prevention policies are sometimes erroneously portrayed as not really getting down to the roots of the problem. In relatively affluent countries such policies do get down to the roots of the crime problems. They help to reduce the nearly universal and still growing opportunities for crime in the emerging urban jungles of today's metropolis. Criminologists and politicians should finally acknowledge the truth in the near universal saying that «opportunity makes the thief». As another old European proverb says: an open door makes a thief of a holy man[28]. Limiting opportunities of crime means nothing less than preventing underprivileged young people from becoming thieves by closing the doors of crime. In the final analysis, situational crime prevention is not just a matter of rational choices but of moral responsibility too.

NOTES

1.   I want to thank John van Kesteren and Leo Toornvliet of the Criminological Institute of the University of Leyden for their support in analysing the data and Pat Mayhew of the Home Office, UK and many others for their support in carrying out the ICS's.

2.   The data on Papua New Guinea and Hungary are not available on diskette and therefore not included in the regional rates and the other analyses.

3.   Data on educational attainment and GNP per capita were taken from the UNDP Report 1992.

4.   According to the United Nations Development report (UNDP, 1992) Japan and the Netherlands are the nations with the smallest inequalities in human development.

5.   Following the terminology of Becker (1968) and other economists, Balkin and McDonald (1980) and Cook (1986) refer to the offenders as the suppliers of offenses. This logically brings them to referring to the victims as persons «demanding» their victimisation. The obvious criticism raised against such models is that there is no demand of being victimised (Cusson, 1990; Clarke and Felson, 1993). In the present model we propose a related interactionist model which does not, however, feature the victims as the demanding party, but as the reluctant supplier of opportunities. In general we will follow less closely the economists' model of market theory and try to bring together insights from existing economic and criminological theories.

6.   The opportunity costs of habitual offending are lowest for unemployed persons. Since the drawing of social benefits is not affected by a persons's involvement in crime, the level of state benefits seems criminologically less relevant than the rate of unemployed adolescents and the level of minimum wages.

7.   Although it is difficult to determine the monetary equivalent of feelings of remorse or of social stigmatisation, moral inhibitions to offend can in principle be included in the costs equation.

8.   The rational interactionist model does not assume that involvement in criminal activity is exclusively affected by economic adversity and the frequency of offending exclusively by criminal opportunities. Both the participation in criminal activity and the frequency of offending are determined by both factors. The potential victims respond to the total number of crimes.

9.   Unemployed or otherwise socially deprived youngsters in the most affluent and egalitarian societies may be more resentful about their situation than objectively more deprived youngsters elsewhere because of a starker contrast between political ideology and actual practice (Stack, 1982; Jongman en Timmerman, 1985).

10.   According to the model high levels of crime generate a heightened risk awareness. This mental state may or may not be accompanied by emotions of fear. In accordance with the literature we will refer to heightened risk awareness as fear of crime.

11.   The widespread implementation of anti-burglary measures among a high risk population reduces their rates of burglaries, but this effect will not undo the positive relation between burglary rates and ownership of anti-burglary devices.

12.   Victimisation rates of cities or neighbourhoods do not include victimisations of visitors and area rates of offenses do not include offenses committed elsewhere.

13.   The ICS contained questions on income of the household and on the age of leaving school. It proved difficult to determine the dollar equivalents of income in third world countries. In theory the data on educational level should be comparable. In many developing countries, though, the percentages of «don't know» answers were too high.

14.   The item on income satisfaction was not yet included in the first ICS. This information is therefore missing for a quarter of the (industrialised) regions. For those regions the average ratio between satisfied and dissatisfied young males was applied to the rates of young males. These regions were given an estimated value instead of a measured value. All relevant analyses were repeated with missing values for the latter regions. In all instances the analyses showed similar results as the analyses using estimated values.

15.   In those regions where the new item was missing, the old item was included. The relationships with victimisation rates would probably have been stronger if information on recreational outdoor visits had been available for all regions.

16.   The difference between the number of structural parameters in the path models and the number of correlations of observed variables is expressed by the number of degrees of freedom (d.f.). The d.f. value is higher to the extent that the causal model is more economical than the full matrix of correlations. The X^2 value indicates the loss of information relative to the matrix. In principle the X^2 value must not be larger than the d.f. value.

17.   The variable *social inequality* (SDSES) is inversely related to *affluence* (-.25) but also unrelated to overall *victimisation* (-0.05).

18.   Among Western countries national beer consumption rates and national rates for threats/assaults are weakly correlated (rank order correlation .434; p<10; n=18; Van Dijk and Mayhew, 1993). In the path model of industrialised countries threats/assaults were related to an outgoing lifestyle too (Bêta .223).

19.   In the literature on urban crime some authors have assumed that crime rates are driven up by a vicious spiral of victimisation experiences, fear of crime and avoidance behaviour. According to this view crime undermines social control by

increasing the mobility of tenants and diminishing the use of public space (Conklin, 1975; Wilson, Kelling, 1982; Skogan, Maxfield, 1981). In some crime ridden neighbourhoods fear of crime may indeed undermine social cohesion and control, especially if such neighbourhoods become pockets of the elderly and the dispossessed. At the level of cities and regions, however, high levels of risk awareness will, in our view, help to stabilise crime.

20.   In his cross-national comparative study Bennett (1991) found that, although development level positively affects theft rates, the impact ends at a threshold point. He interprets this non-linear relationship as suggesting that at high developmental levels adaptive social mechanism — such as target hardening and neighbourhood watch — begin to alter the outcomes. The rational interactionist model assumes that crime is affected by self-protection at all levels and not necessarily at the highest levels only. Possibly increased self-protection has more impact in affluent, high crime countries than elsewhere. The saturation or threshold effect might also be the result of 'saturated' reporting and police recording in the latter countries.

21.   The Japanese police collects information on the motives of arrested perpetrators of crimes. A recent report shows that the proportions of crimes committed for covering living expenses or to prevent bankruptcy declined since 1979 and that the proportion of crimes committed for «pleasure» or «greedy purposes» had gone up (National Police Agency 1992).

22.   The variable urbanisation is itself related to 'motivation' and 'affluence' and inversely related to 'motivation'. As explained earlier a high degree of urbanisation is in our data-set strongly associated with developing countries because of the sampling design. Inclusion of urbanisation in the analysis produced results which were difficult to interpret.

23.   Similar factor analyses were carried out on regional rates (N=156). The factor structures found were largely identical to those found in the analysis of the national rates, but somewhat less clear cut.

24.   Final statistics after varimax rotation

	value	pct. var. exp.	tot. pct. var. exp.
factor 1	5.07	33.9	33.9
factor 2	3.29	21.9	55.8
factor 3	1.83	12.2	68.0
factor 4	1.44	9.6	77.6
factor 5	.76	5.0	82.6

25.   In the first analysis, the variable sexual incidents also showed a high loading on this factor. Since this type of crime is a heterogeneous mixture of domestic violence and sexual harassment by outsiders, it seems to call for a separate analysis. At this stage we have excluded it from the factor analysis.

26.   The stabilisation of crime in the USA has been interpreted as the result of the punitive sentencing policies introduced in the late seventies. This interpretation is less plausible, since the large majority of prisoners have been convicted for drugs offenses or violent offenses rather than for property offenses. Unlike property offenses, drugs offenses and violent offenses have continued to rise in the USA.

27.   In 1993 and 1994 the International Crimes against Businesses Survey was carried out in ten countries. Preliminary results will shortly be released. With some exceptions the ranking of countries on the basis of the ICBS-victimisation rates is identical to the ICS ranking. Investments in business security tend to reflect the levels of crime.

28.   In German: Offene Tür verführt einen Heiligen; in Spanish: puerta abierta al santo tenta; and in Dutch: De open deur roept den dief (Cats).

BIBLIOGRAPHY

Balkin, Steven and John F. McDonald (1981) The Market for Street Crime: An Economic Analysis of Victim-Offender Interaction. In: Journal of Urban Economics, vol. 10, pp. 390-405.

Bartel, Ann (1975) An Analysis of Firm Demand for Protection against Crime. In: Journal of Legal Studies, 4, June, pp. 443-478.

Becker, G.S. (1968) Crime and punishment: an econometric theory. In: Journal of Political Economy, 70, February.

Belknap, Joanne E. (1989) The economics-crime link. Criminal Justice Abstracts, vol. 21, no. 1, pp. 140-157.

Bennett, Trevor (1990) Tackling fear of crime. Home Office Research and Statistics Department. Research Bulletin, vol. 31, no. 28, pp. 14-19.

Bennett, Richard (1991) Development and Crime. A Cross-National, Time-Series Analysis of Competing models. The Sociological Quarterly, vol. 32, no. 3, pp. 343-363.

Bonger, W.A. (1905) Criminalité et conditions économiques/criminality and economic conditions, trans. Henry P. Horton. Boston: Little Brown, 1919.

Braithwaite, John (1989) The State of Criminology: Theoretical Decay or Renaissance. In: Australian and NZ Journal of Criminology, vol. 22, pp. 129-135.

Ching-Chi Hsieh and M.D. Pugh (1993) Poverty Income Inequality and Violent Crime: A Meta-Analysis of Recent Aggregate Data Studies, Criminal Justice Review, vol. 18, no. 2, Autumn.

Chiricos, Theodore G. (1987) Rates of crime and unemployment: an analysis of aggregate research evidence. Social Problems, vol. 34, no. 2, pp. 187-212.

Clarke, Ronald V. (1980) Situational Crime Prevention: Theory and Practice. In: British Journal of Criminology, 20, pp. 130-147.

Clarke, Ronald V. and Marcus Felson (1993) Routine Activity and Rational Choice, Advances in Criminological Theory, vol. 5, New Brunswick, NJ: Transaction.

Clarke, Ronald V. (1994), Crime Prevention Studies, vol. 2, Monsey, New York, Criminal Justice Press.

Clotfelter, C.T. (1977) Urban Crime and Household Protective Measures. In: Review of Economics and Statistics, 59, pp. 499-503.

Cohen, Lawrence E. and Marcus Felson (1979) Social Change and crime rate trends: a routine activity approach. American Sociological Review, vol. 44, pp. 588-608.

Cohen, Stanley (1990) Intellectual Doubts and Political Certainties: the Case of Radical Criminology, Amsterdam: Stichting W.A. Bonger Lezingen.

Cornish, Derek B. and Ronald V. Clarke (eds.) (1986) The reasoning criminal: rational choice perspectives on offending. New York: Springer Verlag.

Conklin, John E. (1975) The Impact of Crime. New York; London: Macmillan; Collier Macmillan.

Cook, Philip J. (1986) The demand and supply of criminal opportunities. In: Michael Tonry and Norval Morris (eds.) Crime and Justice, vol. 9. Chicago: University of Chicago Press, pp. 1-27.

Cusson, Maurice (1990) Croissance et décroissance du crime. Paris: Presses Universitaires de France.

Cusson, Maurice (1993) L'effet structurant du contrôle social, In: Criminologie, Vol. XXVI, no. 2, pp. 37-63.

Del Frate, Anna, Ugi Zvekic and Jan J.M. van Dijk (1993) Understanding Crime; Experiences of Crime and Crime control, Rome: UNICRI.

Erbès, J.M. (1991) Avant-propos, La mésure de la délinquance. In: Les cahiers de la Securité Interieure, Paris, IHESI, no. 4, février-avril.

Farrell, Graham and Ken Pease (1993) Once Bitten, Twice Bitten: Repeat victimisation and its Implications for Crime Prevention. London: Home Office Police Research Group.

Felson, Marcus (1994) Crime and Everyday Life: Insight and Implications for Society. Thousand Oaks: Pine Forge Press.

Field, Simon and Tim Hope (1989) Economics, the consumer and under-provision in crime prevention. Home Office, Research and Planning Unit, Research Bulletin, no. 26, pp. 20-44.

Field, Simon (1990) Trends in crime and their interpretation: a study of recorded crime in post war England and Wales. London: HMSO.

Forrester, David et al (1990) The Kirkholt burglary prevention project: phase II London: Home Office, Crime Prevention Unit.

Heiland, Hans-Gunther and Louise Shelley (1992). Civilization, Modernisation and the Development of Crime and Control. In: Crime Control and Comparative Perspectives. Berlin: Walter de Gruyter.

Heineke, J.M. (1978) Economic Models of Criminal Behavior. Amsterdam: North Holland Pub. Company.

Hesseling, René B.P. (1994) Displacement: a Review of the Empirical Literature. In: R. Clarke (ed.). Crime Prevention Studies, vol. 2, Monsey, New York, Criminal Justice Press.

Hirschi, T. and M. Gottfredson (1983) Age and the explanation of crime. American Journal of Criminology, vol. 89, nr. 3, pp. 552-584.

Hirschi, T. (1969) Causes of Delinquency. Berkeley: University of California Press.

Human Development Report 1992 (1992) United Nations Development Programma, New York, Oxford University Press.

Jongman, R.W. en H. Timmerman (1985) Criminaliteit als verzet: motivatie en remmingen. Tijdschrift voor Criminologie, vol. 27, no. 5, pp. 303-319.

Jöreskog, K.G. and D. Sörbom (1983) Lisrel VI Users Guide, Uppsala: Department of Statistics, University.

Lindsay, Betsy and Daniel McGillis (1986) Citywide community crime prevention: an assessment of the Seattle program. In: P. Rosenbaum (ed) Community Crime prevention: does it work. Beverly Hills: Sage, pp. 68-86.

Liska, Allen E. and Barbara D. Warner, Functions of Crime: a Paradoxical Process. In: American Journal of Sociology, vol. 96, no. 6, pp. 1441-63.

Lynch, James P. (1993) Secondary Analysis of International Crime Survey Data. In: Del Frate, Anna Alvazzi; Ugljesa Zvekic and Jan J.M. van Dijk (eds.) (1993) Understanding Crime: Experiences of Crime and Crime Control. Rome: UNICRI, pp. 175-189.

Mayhew, Pat et al. (1976) Crime as Opportunity, London: Home Office.

Mayhew, Pat (1990) Opportunity and Vehicle Crime In: D.M. Gottfredson and V.C. Clarke (eds), Policy and theory in criminal justice: contributions in honour of Leslie T. Wilkins aldershot: Gower.

Merton, R.F. (1957) Social Theory and Social Structure, Glencoe: The Free Press.

National Police Agency (1992), White Paper on Police, 1992 (excerpt), Tokyo: The Japan Times.

Norström, Thor (1988) Theft Criminality and Economic Growth. Social Science Research, vol. 17, pp. 48-65.

Petersilia, Joan (1991) Policy relevance and the future of criminology: the American Society of Criminology. Criminology, vol. 29, nr. 1, pp. 1-14.

Runciman, W.G. (1972) Relative Deprivation and Social Justice. Middlesex: Penguin.

Saris, W.E. (1984) Causal Modelling in Non-experimental Research: an Introduction to the Lisrel Approach. Amsterdam: Sociometric Research Foundation.

Shickor, David (1990) Crime Patterns and Socioeconomic Development: a cross-national analysis. In: Criminal Justice Review, vol. 15, no. 1 , Spring.

Siemaszko, Andrej (1992). Review of Selected Research. In: Development and Crime, An Exploratory Study in Yugoslavia. Rome: UNICRI.

Skogan, Wesley G. (1987) The impact of victimisation on fear. Crime and Delinquency, vol. 33, nr. 1, pp. 135-154.

Skogan, Wesley G. and Michael G. Maxfield (1981) Coping with crime: individual and neighborhood reactions. Beverly Hills: Sage.

Skogan, Wes (1991) Trends in Crime in the United States. In: International Forum on Crime Prevention, Tokyo: JUSRI.

Stack, Steven (1982) Social structure and Swedish crime rates: a time-series analysis, 1950-1959, Criminology, vol. 20, 3/4, pp. 499-513.

Sutherland, E.H. and D.R. Cressey (1966) Principles of Criminology. Philadelphia: Lippincott.

Svensson, Bo (1986) Welfare and Criminality in Sweden. In: Kevin Heal and Gloria Laycock (eds.) Situational Crime Prevention: from Theory into Practice. London: HMSO, pp. 113-122.

Takasugi, Fumiko (1991) The present and future of Japan's crime: from a structural analysis of victimisation rates. In: G. Kaiser, H. Kury and H.J. Albrecht (eds.) Victims and criminal justice: victimological research: stocktaking and prospects. Freiburg: Max-Planck-Institut, pp. 469-510.

Thomas, G.C. and D. Edelman (1988) evaluation of Conservative Crime Control Theology. Notre Dame Law Review, vol. 63, no. 2, pp. 123-160.

United Nations Office in Vienna (1992) Crime Trends and Criminal Justice Operations at the Regional and Interregional Level. New York: UN Publication.

United Nations Development Programme (1992) Human Development Report 1992. New York/Oxford: Oxford University Press.

Van Dijk, Jan J.M. and Carl Steinmetz (1979), De WODC slachtofferenquêtes, 1973-1979 (report on the Dutch National Crime Surveys 1973-1979), Den Haag: WODC.

Van Dijk, Jan J.M. (1990) On the uses of the international crime survey. In: International forum on crime prevention 1990. Tokyo: Japan Urban Security Research Institute, pp. 90-104.

Van Dijk, Jan J.M., Pat Mayhew and Martin Killias (1990) Experiences of crime across the world: key findings of the 1989 International Crime Survey. Deventer: Kluwer Law and Taxation.

Van Dijk, Jan J.M. (1991) Criminaliteit als keerzijde: een theoretische en empirische verkenning van de relaties tussen welvaart en criminaliteit. Arnhem: Gouda Quint.

Van Dijk, Jan J.M. and Pat Mayhew (1993) Criminal Victimisation in the Industrialised World: Key Findings of the 1989 and 1992 International Crime Surveys. In: Del Frate et.al. (eds.), Understanding Crime, Rome: UNICRI.

Van Dijk, Jan J.M. (1994) Understanding Crime Rates; On the Interactions between the Rational Choices of Victims and Offenders. British Journal of Criminology, Vol. 34, no. 2, Spring.

Van Dijk, Jan J.M. (1994), Who is Afraid of the Crime Victim?, keynote lecture at the VIII Symposium of the World Society of Victimology, Adelaide, 26 August (to be published in the proceedings).

Van Tulder, Frank (1994), Van misdaad tot Straf; van economisch model tot simulatie (From crime to punishment; from economical model to simulation, Ph D thesis), University of Amsterdam.

Von Hirsch, Andrew (1988), Selective incapacitation reexamined: the national academy of sciences report on criminal careers and career criminals. Criminal Justice Ethics, vol. 7, no. 1, pp. 19-35.

Von Hofer, Hanns and Hendrik Thamm (1989), General Deterrence in a longitudinal perspective, a Swedish case: theft, 1984-1985. European Sociological Review, vol. 5, no. 1, pp. 25-45.

Warr, M. (1987) Fear of Crime and Sensitivity to risk. Journal of Quantitative Criminology, vol. 3, nr. 1, pp. 29-46.

Weatherburn, Don (1992) Economic Adversity and Crime. In: Trends and Issues in Crime and Criminal Justice, Australian Institute of Justice, August.

Wilkins, L. World crime: to measure or not to measure. In: Newman, G. (ed), Crime and Deviance: a comparative perspective. Beverley Hills, Sage.

Willemse, Hans (1994) Developments in Dutch Crime Prevention. In: R. Clarke (ed.), Crime Prevention Studies, vol. 2, Monsey, New York, Criminal Justice Press.

Wilson, James Q. and G. Kelling (1982) Broken windows: the police and neighborhood safety. Atlantic Monthly, March, pp. 29-38.

Wikström, Per-Olof and Lars Dolmen (1990) Crime and crime trends in different urban environments. Journal of Quantitative Criminology, vol. 6, no. 1, pp. 7-30.

Winkel, F.W. (1991) Police, victims and crime prevention: some research-based recommendations on victim-oriented interventions. British Journal of Criminology, vol. 31, pp. 250-265.

Young, Jock (1986) The failure of criminology: the needs for a radical realism. In: Roger Matthews and Jock Young (eds.) Confronting crime. London: Sage, pp. 4-30.

CRIME AND ECONOMY

11th Criminological
Colloquium
(1994)

GENERAL REPORT

by
Mr M. JOUTSEN
General Rapporteur,
European Institute
for Crime Prevention and Control,
affiliated with the United Nations (HEUNI)
(Finland)

1. Introduction

The Eleventh Criminological Colloquium has discussed a wide-ranging topic, the interrelationship between crime and the economy. The underlying assumption has been that the development of the economy and businesses cycles have an effect on the amount and structure of crime on one hand, and on the operation of the criminal justice system on the other. The Colloquium has sought to identify these effects, and to see whether they apply equally to the different member States of the Council of Europe, both the Western European member States and the countries in transition in Central and Eastern Europe.

The Colloquium has discussed the subject on the basis of four reports, dealing respectively with «The effects of economic structures and phases of development on crime» (Manuel Eisner, Switzerland), «Economic cycles and crime in Europe» (Simon Field, United Kingdom), «The effect of economic circumstances on the criminal justice system» (Dario Melossi, Italy) and «Opportunities for crime: a test of the rational-interactionist model» (Jan van Dijk, the Netherlands).

The discussion has been lively and has covered a broad spectrum of issues. The participants used the excellent reports as a basis for rigorous questioning of earlier attempts at theory building, and tested the proposed theories against the available data from different countries. Because of the breadth of the topic, many issues could be covered only in passing, and must await fuller development at subsequent meetings. For these reasons, providing a general report on the discussions is in itself a challenging task.

2. Problems with theory-building on crime and the economy

The theories presented at the Colloquium sought to explain developments in crime by referring to changes in the economy. Especially when such theories seek to explain long-term developments in crime and developments in a number of countries, they face the difficulty of a lack of reliable data. Although the theories presented here were careful and perceptive in their use of the data, some general comments on the difficulties they had to overcome may provide a useful frame of reference.

When constructing theories that focus on economic factors such as unemployment, affluence or consumption as independent variables and changes in crime and criminal justice as dependent variables, there is the risk of overlooking other explanatory and intervening factors. Examples are the consumption of alcohol or drugs, the rate of divorce and other sociological phenomena, and the prevalence of firearms. The effect of such factors may in fact override or hide the impact of changes in the economy.

2.1. The limitations of theories based on reported crime

The first problem with the data is that the most widely used source, reported crime, tends to be one-sided. Such data are largely limited to traditional crime (such as property crime and violent crime) at the expense of, for example, economic crime,

149

organised crime and corruption. Reported crime is the result of several filtering processes, changes in priorities and changes in perception and definition which in themselves may be affected by the economy. Also, we know from experience that most crime remains unreported. Moreover, the available data tends to come from the developed, industrialised countries of Western Europe and North America. A more recent source of comparative data, victimization surveys, avoids some of these problems, but involves problems of its own.

2.2.   The use of aggregated data

Second, the data used tends to be aggregated on the national level, and insufficient attention is paid to local differences. It is difficult to adduce from developments on a national level what impact these developments may have on certain groups in society, such as young, urban unemployed males or, for that matter, on the chief executive officers and managers of companies in financial difficulties. Aggregated data may be suitable for macro-level theories, but do not help in testing micro-level theories.

2.3.   The effect of changes in the definition, structure, perception and control of crime

Third, the implicit assumption appears often to be made in economic theories of crime that the definition, structure and perception of crime remains constant, as does the control of crime through formal and informal means. For example, homicides within a family differ from stranger-to-stranger homicides, and homicides committed in the heat of passion differ from homicides committed for gain (for example, from homicides committed in connection with organized crime). It is probable that economic factors have a different impact on crimes committed in different circumstances.

2.4.   The effect of economic factors on the prevalence and incidence of crime

Fourth, macro-level economic theories of crime do not distinguish between the prevalence and incidence of crime. If a theory suggests, for example, that unemployment increases the amount of crime, this does not necessarily mean that a given proportion of the unemployed commit crime. We know from research that a small minority of any birth cohort commits a large share of all offences. Unemployment may promote offending among those who *already* offend, not among those who do not have a propensity to engage in criminal behaviour. A person who has already committed a few burglaries may have a greater propensity to commit further burglaries if he or she becomes unemployed, and a person who is already abusive in a personal relationship may become even more violent when confronted with economic distress.

2.5.   Simplistic mechanical explanations

A related problem is that the existing economic theories of crime generally appear to assume a straightforward mechanical correlation between the variables: an increase of ten percent in unemployment, for example, may lead to an increase of 5 %

in property crime. However, it is possible that unemployment (to use this example) has a differential impact. The first to become unemployed are generally the young and the socially disadvantaged, persons who tend to come from the same pool of persons who are at a high risk of engaging in criminal behaviour. An this stage, an increase in unemployment may indeed at first increase the amount of crime. Should unemployment expand to affect (for example) well-educated middle-class adults with strong social commitment to conforming behaviour, the effect on crime may decrease.

2.6. The selection of variables

Sixth, as already noted, the selection of the variables used in the analysis will affect the results. The theory may neglect to take into consideration potentially important explanatory variables, such as changes in the structure of opportunities (such as the availability of weapons in respect of violent crime), the use of alcohol, the development (or absence of) social welfare provisions and other mechanisms for financial and other support (such as the extended family), relative deprivation and income disparity, and changes in the structure of crime. It may be too ambitious to assume that changes in crime can be explained by one or only a few economy-linked factors. (Life is not as simple as some economists — and some criminologists — may like to think).

The selection of variables is always a deliberate choice. The researcher hypothesises that certain factors can explain the development of crime, and then tests to see whether the data prove or disprove the theory. Ideological blindness, however, may limit the search for alternative explanations. For example, some persons have sought to demonstrate that the amount of crime can be explained simply by the certainty and severity of punishment; when certainty and severity decrease, crime is said to increase. Such theories generally fail to account for changes in the opportunity for crime or other changes in society, and similarly fail to explain why the amount of (reported) crime increases even when the certainty and/or severity of punishment also increases.

2.7. The definition and measure of the economy

Seventh, the «economy» is not an unambiguous concept. Not only can the cultural definition of various measures of economic and social development — such as unemployment, affluence, consumption, inequality — change over time, but reference may also need to be made to the development of the underground or «grey» economy. The distinction between the illegal underground economy and the legal economy is by no means clear.

3. Theories on the links between the economy and crime

Many of the background assumptions of the economic theories of crime rest on a reliable basis. Over the last 200 years, Europe has undergone a period of sustained economic growth. During this period, the relative importance of the primary industries sector has shrunk along with the expansion of the industrial sector and, later, of the service sector. This economic growth has been accompanied by such well-documented

151

processes as urbanisation, an increase in spatial mobility, an expansion of the role of the State, profound demographic changes, a growth in general educational levels, and increasing individualisation and secularisation.

Earlier attempts to invest such factors with explanatory power have raised problems. According to the modernisation thesis, the assumed side-effects of development — social isolation, social disorganisation, a break-down of social control and anomie — contribute to a growth in property crime and violent crime. Variations of this thesis, the life-style model and the routine activity model, focus on the increase in opportunities for crime. The theory of the civilising process, on the other hand, suggests that functional differentiation and increasing mutual interdependence, which accompany modernisation, result in growing external formal control and intensified self-control. This, in turn, should decrease the amount of crime, in particular violent crime. Thus, while the lifestyle and the routine activity models posit that economic development increases the opportunity for crime through, e.g., an increase in the number of targets for property crime (such as cars and consumer goods) and an increase in potential violent interaction with strangers, the civilising process model posits that economic development decreases crime by strengthening formal and internalised control.

3.1.   Economic structure and crime: the case of homicide

A review of patterns in homicide in many Western European countries since the 1800s shows a continuous decrease since about the 1840s to the early 1960s. For the past thirty years, reported homicide rates have been increasing. Similarly, the trend in total reported crime decreased for about a century beginning during the 1840s, and began to increase steeply in the late 1950s. This increase was particularly marked during the 1960s and the 1970s. (As was noted, it cannot be assumed that the structure of these homicides — much less the concept of «total reported crime» — has remained the same over this lengthy period).

In the absence of empirical data from the earlier period, it is not possible to know to what extent the first increase in reported homicide during the early 1800s was due to urbanisation, and to what extent it was due to, for example, improved policing. Furthermore, there are indications from some countries that homicide has been at even higher levels during earlier centuries, such as between the 1400s and the early 1700s. However, the pattern from the 1840s on does not fit in well with the modernisation thesis as generally presented: reported crime decreased for about a century and then increased, by and large in direct opposition to what this thesis would suggest.

A focus on the demand for, and the development of, individual self-control, as suggested in Mr. Eisner's paper, provides new and interesting insights that could help in explaining some of these changes. «Self-control» can be understood as a personal resource with an emotional, strategic and normative component. A person who has self-control is able to express his or her emotions in a culturally acceptable manner, is able to cope reflexively with problems and challenges, and is able to act according to internalised moral rules.

Modernisation (e.g. functional differentiation, urbanisation, the increase in skilled work, the greater variety in lifestyles) has been accompanied by a gradual increase in the level of self-control expected in a given situation, and by changes in the mode of self-control expected. At the same time, more highly integrated social structures, the increase in economic, social and cultural capital (the Taylorist organisation of work, the contractual character of employment, the rigorous time-rhythm of work, the rise of a working-class culture, the emergence of strong political ideologies) and the expansion of compulsory education have provided the individual with the greater self-control required.

Baldly put, from the mid-1800s to the early 1900s, modern society has demanded more self-control of the individual, but it has also indoctrinated the individual to exercise the required amount of self-control.

If the level and mode of self-control expected of the individual exceeds the individual's «supply» of self-control, his or her restraints against committing crime may fail. From about the 1950s on, several factors have increased the amount of self-control necessary in modern society. These factors include

—   the decline in the manufacturing sector and the rise of the service sector,

—   the rise in educational requirements; and

—   the destandardisation of life-courses in education and employment.

At the same time, several factors have combined to erode the ability of the individual to exert the required self-control:

—   the trend towards hedonistic values;

—   the decline of socially integrating networks, in particular the family; and

—   the marginalisation of urban lower-class areas and indeed in some cases of entire regions and countries.

Before the 1950s, little expressive capabilities were required, individual autonomy was not very important, the individual was subordinated to State authority, and the family was based on common interests and a division of labour. Since the 1950s, in turn, expressive capabilities and individual autonomy became more important, leisure-time activities became important for the formation of one's identity, and the family became based more on mutual partnership.

In the case of Central and Eastern Europe, this theory based on self-control may help to explain the sudden increase in reported crime beginning at the end of the 1980s. The fundamental economic, political and social changes have resulted in changes in the mode and amount of self-control required. At the same time, however, the changes have partly destroyed the ability of society to instil the necessary self-control.

Adaption to change in itself requires considerable self-control. When the shift is from a monolithic ideological system to one that stresses a diversity of interests and the principles of free enterprise (misunderstood by many to mean «anything goes»), the increase in self-control that is required may be enormous.

For many persons, the rapid drop in the standard of living, the spread of unemployment and the rising rate of inflation in all Central and Eastern European countries, and the reality (and perception) of increased crime, eroded the barriers that self-control placed on the commission of crime. This erosion presumably increased when people noted that canny entrepreneurs were bending the limits of the law (if not directly overstepping them), and that governments lacked the supervisory and enforcement machinery required to oversee that the new legislation works as it should. The formal and informal controls that strengthen self-control appeared to be missing.

The theory based on self-control appears to fit in well with the U-shaped curve in reported crime (in this case, homicide, with only spotty data available on total reported crime trends up to the 1990s) over the past 150 years: at first a gradual decline in crime, followed by an increase since the middle of this century. The theory was, however, subjected to considerable criticism at the Colloquium. First, the use of reported homicide as an indicator was faulted on the grounds that the year-to-year variations are too small to provide an adequate test of the theory. More generally, reported crime has many sources of error. Some argued that it is not a reliable indicator of an increase in, and later loss of, self-control.

Second, other and simpler factors were suggested as having a stronger impact on crime rates, in particular over the past decades: country-specific examples are the consumption of alcohol and drugs, and the use of firearms. It was argued that these simpler factors should first be discounted before explaining any remaining variation, or that they should at least be woven into the theory.

Third, «self-control» as a concept needs to be further analysed. It was noted that, in some environments, strong self-control can in fact help to socialise the individual into criminal subcultures or organisations. (Essentially, being a successful criminal in a criminal environment requires considerable self-control.) The theory as it has been presented is thus not a satisfactory tool for dealing with, for example, economic crime or organised crime.

Nonetheless, the theory raises many important and thought-provoking issues, and can be considered an improvement over the earlier modernisation and civilising process theories. It requires further refining, tests on the basis of better data, and tests using data from different countries.

3.2.   Economic cycles and crime

According to the economic theory of crime, potential offenders allocate their time to a mix of legal and illegal activities, depending on the risks and rewards associated with each. In good years, when spending increases, the motivation for crime is less (the motivational effect). On the other hand, when spending increases and there are more «targets» for crime available, the opportunity for crime also increases (the opportunity effect). In times of recession, when people are thrown out of work and have only a limited ability to earn income through legitimate activity, the motivation to commit crime may increase.

An analysis by Mr. Field of crime rates in England and Wales suggests that a distinction must be made between crime for gain (primarily property crime) and crime not undertaken for gain (such as assault and sexual offences). The data suggest that when spending increases in good years (as measured by consumption), reported crime for gain (as measured by property crime) at first rises more slowly or even falls, but reported crime not for gain increases at an accelerating pace. This may be due to the predominance of the motivational effect over the opportunity effect, with the motivational effect being directed through the relatively small group of young males who are responsible for most recorded crime. Overall, it appeared that consumption was more closely associated with reported crime trends than was unemployment.

Although an attempt to replicate these results with data from the United States provided strong confirmation of the theory, an analysis of data from other Western European countries only provided weak confirmation of a relationship between business cycles and crime. Nonetheless, the results did indicate that where such a relationship is confirmed, it follows the lines noted in England and Wales.

The criticism of this theory was based on the weak fit of the theory to the data available from outside England and Wales. Simply put, the criticism holds that since the theory does not match the data, the theory must be wrong. However, the fit between the data on consumption and the data on property crime in England and Wales as well as the United States was so remarkably strong that further exploration of the theory is called for.

Several explanations for the poor explanatory power of the theory in respect of data from other Western European countries were advanced. These other societies may have cushioned the impact of a recession through the development of a welfare society, thus softening the effect of decreases in consumption. It is also possible that the INTERPOL data used in the analysis are misleading due to a different classification of offences, and a more rigorous data-collection exercise would be required for each country analysed. A third possible explanation is that there are large differences between the countries in respect of the opportunity for crime, which again would soften the impact of changes in consumption on property crime.

A fourth factor that was raised focused on the differential impact of the business cycle on the small, crime-prone group of young males in urban areas. It is possible that there are large differences in the changes in motivation of this group in England and Wales as well as the United States on one hand, and in the other Western European countries examined on the other. Furthermore, it is possible that a multivariate analysis that includes not only consumption but also such factors as unemployment and the proportion of this group out of the total population may make sense out of the developments on Continental Europe — West, Central and Eastern.

3.3. Opportunities and crime

The results of the two sweeps of the international victimisation surveys appear to refute the widely assumed existence of a simple unilinear relationship between modernisation (affluence) and (property) crime. High crime rates are to be found in both developed and developing countries; indeed, the crime rates in some of the large cities in developing countries by and large exceed those of corresponding cities in developed countries.

As noted by Mr. van Dijk, in a paper with close parallels to that of Mr Field, this suggests the need for a closer look at the motivation («demand») and opportunity («supply») factors referred to above. More specifically, it can be hypothesised that an increase in affluence leads to (1) a decrease in the motivation to commit an offence, (2) an increase in the opportunity for crime, for example in the availability of cars, targets for theft and the potential for stranger-to-stranger contacts without social control, and (3) a decrease in family cohesion and informal social control.

From the point of view of potential victims, it can be hypothesised that an increase in the motivation to commit an offence, an increase in the opportunity for crime, and a decrease in family cohesion and informal social control all lead to an increase in victimisation. An increase in victimisation, in turn, leads to an increase in fear of crime, which is related to increased use of preventive mechanisms, i.e. self-help in protecting their property and themselves. It can be hypothesised that the level of crime tends to stabilise at the intersection of the demand and supply curves. It is at this point where (potential) victims assume that the marginal cost of added protection would outweigh the marginal loss from the crime prevented.

An analysis of the data from the two sweeps of the international victimisation survey showed, for example, that affluence tends to reduce the motivation to commit crimes, but at the same time tends to increase the opportunity to do so (with the exception of robbery). Car vandalism in particular appears to be an opportunity-driven crime which increases along with affluence.

The discussion of these results touched lightly on many themes dealt with at earlier Council of Europe meetings, such as the establishment of crime prevention councils, the need for data on victimisation of businesses, and the need to include questions in victimisation surveys on costs of crime and the use of self-protection measures.

One provocative point that merits closer inspection is the argument that excessive government intervention in crime prevention decreases private initiative in self-protection. In modern society, the public gradually comes to assume that crime prevention and control is a matter for the government (above all, for the police), and reacts to perceived increases in crime by calling for more police and greater police powers, and for greater government investment in prevention. The police, in turn, may come to adopt the same attitude. They regard themselves as the experts in crime, and discourage the «interference» of untrained members of the public.

It is clear that effective crime prevention and control inevitably require active participation of the public and strong informal social control. However, reallocation of the burden of responsibility between the police and the public raises difficult problems. In part, such reallocation may be construed (correctly or incorrectly) as an attempt by the formal criminal justice system to pass on part of the financial burden of the control of crime in times of financial austerity, as well as to pass on the political blame for failures in crime control in times of increasing crime. Such reallocation may also raise questions of equity: not all can afford to pay for personal crime prevention measures, and the burden of crime may increase on those who are already socially disadvantaged.

Such ideological arguments notwithstanding, the common sense of the public should not be ignored. Many crime prevention measures do not require considerable time, expense and bother. When the risk of (and the fear of) victimisation increases, the public will be more receptive to advice on how to prevent crime. Policy makers should consider methods of encouraging such self-help.

4.   Economy and the criminal justice system

In the discussion of the interrelationship between the economy and the criminal justice system, which was based on the paper by Mr. Melossi, the focus was on punishment, in particular on imprisonment. A distinction was made between the quality of punishment (essentially, the method of treatment of offenders) and the quantity of punishment. Not only are there different denominators of imprisonment (or of any other form of punishment), it is difficult to compare «punitiveness» across time or across jurisdictions.

The concept of severity is, furthermore, related to the perception of the courts and of the public of the seriousness of different acts and the penal value of individual units of punishment. This public perception evolves over time. In respect of the «criminalisation» of behaviour, for example, the public is apparently redefining broad categories of behaviour previously regarded as «a private matter» (e.g. domestic violence), as behaviour that should be subjected to formal sanctions. The public perception may also vary on an almost day-to-day basis, depending on the type of information provided to the public. For example dramatic incidents of crime may lead to a condemnation of an entire category of offences and to demands for increased punishment. In this respect, politicians and legislators were described as «anxiety barometers» who engage in symbolic rhetoric in response to perceived crime problems.

After many decades of decreasing or stable rates of imprisonment, there has been a general increase and change in the use of imprisonment in Western Europe since the early 1970s. The increase in the use of imprisonment appears to be due more to longer stays than to a greater number of admissions to prison. Three categories of inmates in particular have grown in importance: persons awaiting trial, persons sentenced for drug-related crimes, and aliens. Some observers have suggested that imprisonment has now become a «growth industry», and that there are vested economic interests in continued expansion of the prison population.

Changes in the use of imprisonment have at various times been associated with changes in crime rates, changes in the legal status of certain offences (such as drug offences), demographic change, policy change, cultural change (including a growing punitiveness towards deviant behaviour), and with the «self-regulation» of prison systems. Although changes in the use of imprisonment are perhaps most popularly regarded as being related to the first of these factors, changes in crime rates, this has rarely been noted directly. Many examples can be cited of periods from many countries where decreasing crime rates were accompanied by increasing prison rates, and vice versa.

As noted by Mr Melossi, a correlation has been found in many countries between changes in the economy and changes in imprisonment rates. Moreover, these changes have generally been simultaneous, without there being the possibility of the general crime rate serving as the intervening variable between the economy and imprisonment. This appears to be related to two different types of reasons, not independent from each other: 1) that the status of being unemployed appears to be significantly associated with a higher risk of incarceration, something which is particularly clear from individual-level data; 2) that the likelihood of being incarcerated seems to vary not only according to «individual» variables, such as class, race, gender, or status of employment, but also according to specific economic conjunctures and the degree of «moral panic» associated with a specific conjuncture.

In the downswing of an economic cycle — especially if we consider long cycles of 40-50 years — the demand for greater social order and stability seems to express itself also through a demand for «social discipline», therefore also for more aggressive penal policies. The contrary happens in the upswing of the cycle. This is of course something which is culturally mediated, rather than a direct product of economic necessities and/or interests.

5.   The special case of the Central and Eastern European countries

The data presented at the Colloquium were overwhelmingly taken from the developed market economy countries of Western Europe and North America. This raised the question of to what extent the theories being discussed were applicable in the countries of transition in Central and Eastern Europe, where there has been a very rapid and fundamental change in economic structure.

With due regard to the considerable differences between the countries, the economy in the nine Central and Eastern Europe member States of the Council of Europe had traditionally been under much tighter State control than had the economy in Western European countries. The planned economy countries relied on criminal law more than had the market economy countries. For example, these countries had had in force penal provisions that criminalised the operation of private manufacturing and business enterprises, the purchasing and reselling of goods for profit, and the allocation of material and financial resources in contravention to official plans. Imprisonment was possible for the contravention of price regulations and the charging of higher rates of interest.

The present transition thus requires extensive amendment of criminal law and the development of new forms of administrative and commercial regulation. At the same time, the introduction of a new economic system opens up new possibilities of abuse: damage to property owned by the State, the people or by groups of persons entrusted with the administration of such property; tax evasion; unfair competition; credit fraud; and crimes related to capital investment, fraudulent advertising, cheque and credit card abuse, dishonest insider dealing and stock exchange speculation.

During the period of planned economy and during the present process of rapid change, the links between the economy and crime could well be quite different from what could be discerned in the Western European countries. For example, the strength and scope of the underground economy in Central and Eastern Europe has few counterparts in the West. Regrettably, the Colloquium did not provide an opportunity to examine such important issues.

In other respects, the differences may be more one of scale than of substance. The economic changes have affected the opportunities for crime, the motivation to commit crime, and the effectiveness of guardianship. Moreover, the present economic changes affect the standard of living as well as expectations members of the public have regarding victimisation, and their perception of the seriousness of different offences. Given the extent of the problem of crime in Central and Eastern Europe, these issues require separate examination.

6.   Issues for further research and discussion

The topic of the economy and crime was so vast that not all issues could be covered. Organised crime, corruption, economic crime and the role of the underground economy are only some examples of the relevant issues that could not be discussed except in passing.

Although the connection between economic adversity and punitiveness was mentioned, the Colloquium was not able to enter into the complex issue of the possible connection between economic adversity, ethnic violence and hate crimes. This was presumably due to the absence of micro-studies on the perpetrators of such offences. The conjecture is that many violent offenders who target foreigners and members of minorities try to neutralise their behaviour by scapegoating such persons as being responsible for hard economic times.

The related theme of economic change and the status of aliens also deserves separate attention. Many aliens enter a country for purely economic reasons, as «guest workers» and so-called economic refugees. In times of economic upswing, they appear to be largely accepted, albeit grudgingly. In poor economic times, as at the present, there appears to be a tendency to «criminalise» immigrants. This is suggested by the increasing numbers of foreigners held in custody on both criminal and administrative grounds. The economic factors behind these changes have yet to be studied.

The link between the economy and the certainty and severity of punishment was also not addressed in the discussions. As was noted, some theories have sought to show that potential offenders engage in cost-benefit analysis by weighing the potential profit from the offence against the possibility of punishment, and the resulting costs. Given the attractiveness of simple theories to many members of the public (especially if these theories appear to argue for a more punitive response to crime), it would be worthwhile to subject such theories to cool analysis in order to demonstrate the extent to which they accord with the available data. It would also be worthwhile to examine the economic and other costs to society of increased punitiveness, and weigh this against the actual benefits of such a policy in terms of reduced crime.

The connections between economic change and rationalisation of the criminal justice system were another wide area that was left to future discussion. Unless fundamental legal change is carried out (changes in substantive and procedural law, and changes in sentencing provisions) an overburdened criminal justice system reacts to the laws of supply and demand through self-regulation. If resources suddenly become available, these will be used (although not necessarily in the way that the policy-makers had intended). On the other hand, if resources are cut (as is more commonly the case), new priorities will be set and alternative arrangements will be made. The present trend in privatisation, with all the difficulties involved, is largely a result of the play of economic laws in criminal justice.

The length of this list of subjects for future discussion and research illustrates the success of the Eleventh Criminological Colloquium. The combined active input of economists and criminologists from East and West, Northern and Southern Europe resulted in a rich debate where old theories were rejected, new theories were advanced and criticised, and new directions were blazed. In an increasingly integrated Europe beset by fundamental economic changes, the interrelationship between the economy and crime must be submitted to regular review.

CRIME AND ECONOMY

11th Criminological
Colloquium
(1994)

CONCLUSIONS AND RECOMMENDATIONS

by
Mr M. JOUTSEN
General Rapporteur,
European Institute
for Crime Prevention and Control,
affiliated with the United Nations (HEUNI)
(Finland)

CONCLUSIONS

The Eleventh Criminological Colloquium discussed a wide-ranging topic, the interrelationships between the economy and crime. The underlying assumption was that the development of the economy and the operation of business cycles had an effect on the amount and structure of crime on one hand, and on the operation of the criminal justice system on the other. The Colloquium sought to identify these effects, and to see whether they applied generally to the different member States of the Council of Europe, both the Western European States with an established market economy and the countries in transition in Central and Eastern Europe.

Few statements and hypotheses by the rapporteurs or the participants were accepted without challenge. In particular, the participants were rigorous in their examination of any attempts at theory-building, and called for indications of how the facts fit the theories presented. It was also noted that the economy, social development and culture were so interlinked that it would be difficult, if not impossible, to dissect what impact changes in the economy alone had on crime and criminal justice.

It was generally agreed that the traditional theories of the interrelationship between crime and the economy — the modernisation theory, opportunity theory and civilisation theory — fail to explain overall changes in crime in Europe over the past two hundred years.

With due caution regarding methodological difficulties (as noted in the general report), it appeared in the light of the data discussed that overall rates of reported crime in Europe were predominantly determined by the motivation to offend, lifestyle and exposure to crime, the degree of affluence and equality of distribution of income in society, and the degree of urbanisation, all factors which are to a considerable extent measurable with economic indicators. The cohesion of family life and the extent of natural surveillance appear to be secondary determining factors. In the longer term, it was suggested that changes in motivation and opportunity could be linked to changes in the gap between socially required self-control and individual self-control «resources». This theory has interesting implications that merit closer attention.

Results of victimisation surveys indicated that, at a certain level, increases in the opportunity for crime appear to make the potential victims more aware of the risks and of the need for additional precautions. Simple economic theory suggested that a general equilibrium was reached when the marginal cost of protection is greater than the marginal loss through crime. This, understandably, is largely a question of how the individual victim perceives the costs and potential loss.

The discussion on the impact of the economy on the criminal justice system focused on the use of imprisonment. In this connection, problems in analysis were caused by the fact that the quantity and quality of imprisonment varied over time and place; punitiveness is culturally relative. These problems notwithstanding, the data presented at the Colloquium suggested that the use of imprisonment did not correlate markedly well with crime rates, but more for example with the rate of unemployment.

This raises the possibility, already noted in the literature, that imprisonment is in effect being used as a method of segregating the surplus work force — remarkably often aliens — from society. Although great variation was noted in this respect between countries, it was suggested that changes in the economy had an effect on the perception that practitioners in the criminal justice system had of the danger presented by offenders. Economic change may lead to changes in the cultural and ideological climate (as reflected for example in political rhetoric), which in turn affect the sentencing patterns.

While a punitive response to crime, as measured by the use of imprisonment, appeared to have wide support among the population in some countries (which often appear to be countries where crime is demand-driven, i.e. committed out of need), it was doubtful whether more punitive criminal policies could substantially and permanently reduce crime by deterring potential offenders — certainly not without very significant increases in cost. In particular, research suggested that the certainty and severity of punishment had less of an impact on young offenders than on adult offenders.

RECOMMENDATIONS

In general, the subject of the Colloquium does not lend itself to direct recommendations on criminal policy. Much of the Colloquium was devoted to seeking a better understanding of the inter-play between economic development and crime. Furthermore, recommendations on, for example, more balanced economic development and fuller employment need not be made on crime prevention grounds alone. Member States are already highly concerned with such issues. In addition, much of what could be recommended in this connection has already been embodied in, for example, Recommendation N° (87) 19 on the organisation of crime prevention and Recommendation N° R (87) 21 on assistance to victims and the prevention of victimisation. Nonetheless, some recommendations can and should be made in the light of the discussions at the Colloquium, although they do not cover the full scope of the topic.

Crime prevention

1.   The group that appears to be at the highest risk of being negatively affected by changes in the economy (primarily of becoming or remaining unemployed during periods of recession) is the same one that appears to be at the highest risk of committing property and violent offences: socially disadvantaged young males in urban areas as well as persons who have a criminal record. Vocational training and help in achieving social integration are self-evidently necessary in order to avoid permanent marginalisation of large sectors of society.

2.   Specific education, vocation training and social skills training should be developed, as necessary, for aliens and ethnic minorities in order to assist them in meeting the requirements imposed by modern society.

3.   The opportunities for crime can be reduced through increased social guardianship. Governments should support suitable community-based crime prevention initiatives that promote the employment of, for example, caretakers, wardens, conductors and car park attendants as a means of controlling petty crime. Such initiatives would have the additional benefit of creating jobs for low-skilled persons.

4.   Appropriate fiscal policies and statutory measures to encourage potential victims (individuals and corporate bodies) to protect themselves through rational crime prevention measures should be considered. Governments should support in particular economically disadvantaged and vulnerable groups in such self-protection, for example through direct financial and material support and through the promotion of community-based initiatives in social housing projects.

5.   National, regional and local crime prevention councils should co-operate with the local community and for example insurance companies should co-operate with national and regional crime prevention councils in determining reasonable minimum standards of security and in developing a balanced mixture of private and public crime prevention and targeted efforts of the criminal justice system and other government agencies.

International co-operation

6.   The international exchange of information on, and experience with, crime prevention projects related to changes in economic structure and to economic integration should be promoted.

7.   Special attention should be paid to the specific concerns of the new Central and Eastern European member States of the Council of Europe regarding the prevention and control of crime linked with changes in economic structures in Europe. To this end, special assistance should be provided in the form of seminars, study visits and expert meetings.

Future research and other activities

8.   The theories of the links between the economy and crime require further elaboration and testing in different cultures, on both the macro and micro level. The Council of Europe should take initiatives to promote further research in particular on the impact of changes in the economy on crimes against businesses.

9.   Further research on the effectiveness and efficiency of situational crime prevention at the levels of individuals, communities and large populations should also be promoted.

10.   The Council of Europe should consider the organisation of a conference on «The effects of economic, social and political transition in Central and Eastern Europe on crime».

Sales agents for publications of the Council of Europe
Agents de vente des publications du Conseil de l'Europe

AUSTRALIA/AUSTRALIE
Hunter publications, 58A, Gipps Street
AUS-3066 COLLINGWOOD, Victoria
Fax: (61) 34 19 71 54

AUSTRIA/AUTRICHE
Gerold und Co., Graben 31
A-1011 WIEN 1
Fax: (43) 1512 47 31 29

BELGIUM/BELGIQUE
La Librairie européenne SA
50, avenue A. Jonnart
B-1200 BRUXELLES 20
Fax: (32) 27 35 08 60

Jean de Lannoy
202, avenue du Roi
B-1060 BRUXELLES
Fax: (32) 25 38 08 41

CANADA
Renouf Publishing Company Limited
1294 Algoma Road
CDN-OTTAWA ONT K1B 3W8
Fax: (1) 613 741 54 39

DENMARK/DANEMARK
Munksgaard
PO Box 2148
DK-1016 KØBENHAVN K
Fax: (45) 33 12 93 87

FINLAND/FINLANDE
Akateeminen Kirjakauppa
Keskuskatu 1, PO Box 218
SF-00381 HELSINKI
Fax: (358) 01 21 44 35

GERMANY/ALLEMAGNE
UNO Verlag
Poppelsdorfer Allee 55
D-53115 BONN
Fax: (49) 228 21 74 92

GREECE/GRÈCE
Librairie Kauffmann
Mavrokordatou 9, GR-ATHINAI 106 78
Fax: (30) 13 83 03 20

HUNGARY/HONGRIE
Euro Info Service
Magyarorszag
Margitsziget (Európa Ház),
H-1138 BUDAPEST
Fax: (36) 1 111 62 16

IRELAND/IRLANDE
Government Stationery Office
4-5 Harcourt Road, IRL-DUBLIN 2
Fax: (353) 14 75 27 60

ISRAEL/ISRAËL
ROY International
PO Box 13056
IL-61130 TEL AVIV
Fax: (972) 349 78 12

ITALY/ITALIE
Libreria Commissionaria Sansoni
Via Duca di Calabria, 1/1
Casella Postale 552, I-50125 FIRENZE
Fax: (39) 55 64 12 57

MALTA/MALTE
L. Sapienza & Sons Ltd
26 Republic Street
PO Box 36
VALLETTA CMR 01
Fax: (356) 246 182

NETHERLANDS/PAYS-BAS
InOr-publikaties, PO Box 202
NL-7480 AE HAAKSBERGEN
Fax: (31) 542 72 92 96

NORWAY/NORVÈGE
Akademika, A/S Universitetsbokhandel
PO Box 84, Blindern
N-0314 OSLO
Fax: (47) 22 85 30 53

PORTUGAL
Livraria Portugal, Rua do Carmo, 70
P-1200 LISBOA
Fax: (351) 13 47 02 64

SPAIN/ESPAGNE
Mundi-Prensa Libros SA
Castelló 37, E-28001 MADRID
Fax: (34) 15 75 39 98

Llibreria de la Generalitat
Rambla dels Estudis, 118
E-08002 BARCELONA
Fax: (34) 34 12 18 54

SWEDEN/SUÈDE
Aktiebolaget CE Fritzes
Regeringsgatan 12, Box 163 56
S-10327 STOCKHOLM
Fax: (46) 821 43 83

SWITZERLAND/SUISSE
Buchhandlung Heinimann & Co.
Kirchgasse 17, CH-8001 ZÜRICH
Fax: (41) 12 51 14 81

BERSY
Route du Manège 60, CP 4040
CH-1950 SION 4
Fax: (41) 27 31 73 32

TURKEY/TURQUIE
Yab-Yay Yayimcilik Sanayi Dagitim Tic Ltd
Barbaros Bulvari 61 Kat 3 Daire 3
Besiktas, TR-ISTANBUL

UNITED KINGDOM/ROYAUME-UNI
HMSO, Agency Section
51 Nine Elms Lane
GB-LONDON SW8 5DR
Fax: (44) 171 873 82 00

**UNITED STATES and CANADA/
ÉTATS-UNIS et CANADA**
Manhattan Publishing Company
468 Albany Post Road
PO Box 850
CROTON-ON-HUDSON, NY 10520, USA
Fax: (1) 914 271 58 56

STRASBOURG
Librairie Kléber
Palais de l'Europe
F-67075 Strasbourg Cedex
Fax: (33) 88 52 91 21

Council of Europe Publishing/Editions du Conseil de l'Europe
Council of Europe/Conseil de l'Europe
F-67075 Strasbourg Cedex
Tel. (33) 88 41 25 81 - Fax (33) 88 41 27 80